LEGAL ISSUES JOURNAL
Volume 8, Issue 1
January 2020

Legal Issues Journal (LIJ) publishes original research on all legal matters affecting justice, equality and other pressing issues for societies. The journal welcomes interdisciplinary work at the intersection of law and other disciplines, such as genetics, biosciences, philosophy, linguistics, neuroscience, medicine, and business.

The Journal publishes original papers, case comments, short reports, debates and book reviews. The Journal also provides important news and interpretation on changes in the legal world and coming trends affecting law, lawyers, and society. Contribution to society, nationally and internationally, is the focus of LIJ.

LIJ uses double-blind peer review process – both the reviewer(s) and the author(s) are anonymous.

ISSN 2516-1210 (Print)
ISSN 2515-9887 (Online)

The United Kingdom Law and Society Association (UKLSA)

www.uklsa.co.uk

Special Issue

Proceedings of

International Conference: Justice in the Genomic and Digital Era

Sep. 6, 2019
Tomsk, Russia

Table of Contents

Forward

Fatos Selita
Executive Publisher

This is a Special Issue on proceedings of *International Conference: Justice in the Genomic and Digital Era,* held on 6 September 2019 in Tomsk Russia.

We are pleased to join efforts with The Accessible Genetics Consortium (TAGC) and other partner institutions for promoting knowledge and developing regulation covering legal, ethical and societal implications of the genomic and digital era.

The genomic and digital era we currently live in has brought implications for justice. There are a number of emerging legal and ethical issues related to misuse of data—genetic and other. These include discrimination for adults and children, in areas such as health, education, crime prevention and employment. These issues now affect a significant part of societies in advanced economies, and are likely to soon affect most people.

Preparing for this era, both in terms of knowledge and legal regulation, requires wide dissemination of knowledge in this field. Society at large need genetic literacy to be able to protect themselves from psychological and other harm stemming from misuse of their genetic information; and key stakeholders need genetic literacy to enable them to understand implications and the urgency of taking action. Genetic and computing are complex sciences and so general knowledge gained through medial and general reading is not sufficient.

In addition, to address legal and ethical implications of such complex fields, expertise from a number of disciplines needs to be combined—making interdisciplinary collaborations and efforts a prerequisite to effective protection.

Moreover, legal and ethical issues related to genetics and technology are not confined within borders of any country. They are instead global and therefore require multinational collaborations and efforts.

The Conference was held to disseminate knowledge on legal, ethical and societal implications of genetics and digitalisation among professionals and students from a number of jurisdictions; to bring together key disciplines; and to inspire thinking, interest and action towards updating the legal protection of people.

Participants included professionals and students from Law, Psychology, Genetics, Biology and Medicine; from a number of countries, including the Russian Federation, the UK, Iran, Kazakhstan, India, France, Nigeria and Germany.

The Conference was one of the series organised by The Accessible Genetics Consortium (TAGC) in collaboration with Institute of Law and Ethics (ILE), International Laboratory for Interdisciplinary Investigations into Individual Differences in Learning (InLab) and the International Center for Research in Human Development (ICRHD).

Privacy of genetic data: issues with legislation and law enforcement in the Russian Federation

Anna Semiakina[1]

Law Institute, Tomsk State University

Summary. This article aims to evaluate the "gray areas" in Russian legislation regulating the activities of medical organizations for the processing of genetic data as personal data. The analysis includes the relevance of the topic for the economy, science, and law in Russia, and current legislation from the perspective of gaps and enforcement issues. The paper also provides brief recommendations for improving legal regulation in the field of genetic data processing and associated risks.

Genetic research in the Russian Federation is gaining its place in the market for high-tech medical services. So, services for assessing the state of health and risks of hereditary diseases, assisting in the planning of a child, determining dietary features, and evaluat-

[1] Corresponding author. Email: siemiakina.anna@mail.ru

ing medications effects are becoming more and more popular and accessible. Genetic clinics provide genetic counselling via Skype, courier picking up genetic material, and receiving results remotely through clients' accounts on clinics' servers. Pharmaceutical companies are showing interest in creating integrated biomedical databases.

In 2018, genetic research expanded markedly in Russia. The Russian company R-Pharm announced plans to build centers for genetic research in conjunction with the Human Longevity Inc. in the US. The Japanese pharmaceutical company Takeda and the Institute of Cytology and Genetics of the Siberian Branch of the Russian Academy of Sciences announced the completion of a joint project - an integrated database that accumulates research data, pathology mechanisms, and treatment results that the company plans to use to develop new drugs. Also, in 2018, the Skolkovo Institute of Science and Technology and the Medical Genetic Research Center signed a memorandum on the CoBrain Analytics project to create a common medical information database based on an analysis of the patient's genetic data.

In addition, there is also interest by the State in carrying out a genetic identification of the population, the development of gene pool screening technology. In 2019, the Government of the Russian Federation approved the Federal Scientific and Technical Program for the Development of Genetic Technologies for 2019–2027. The Russian Government's task of accumulating personal information about citizens is becoming technically feasible following the switching to digital health records – the creation of the Unified State Information System in Healthcare (EGISZ).

In 2017, Federal Law No. 187 "On the Security of Critical Information Infrastructure of the Russian Federation" was adopted, aimed at ensuring the information security of economic entities. In addition, over the past 6 years, by-laws of different authorities have been adopted: decrees of the Government of the Russian Federation (dated July 6, 2015 No. 676, dated February 8, 2018 No.

127, dated May 5, 2018 No. 555, and April 12, 2018 No. 447); Order of the Ministry of Health of Russia dated June 17, 2019 No. 911n; Orders of the Federal Service for Technical and Export Control - hereinafter referred to as FSTEC (dated February 11, 2013 No. 17, dated February 18, 2013 No. 21, dated March 14, 2014 No. 31, dated December 25, 2017 No. 239).

This updating of legislation confirmed that the previously adopted laws (the Federal Law "On the protection of citizens' health", "On personal data", "On information, information technology and the protection of information") lagged behind scientific and technological progress. In particular, the duty of the owners of critical information infrastructure (CII) is to notify the FSTEC about cyberattacks. The FSTEC clarified the requirements for information protection at CII objects, as well as about the list of CII objects to be categorized. A list of information provided to the State system for detecting, preventing, and eliminating the consequences of computer attacks has been compiled, and a procedure for exchanging information with the subject of CII has been determined. The requirements of the Ministry of Health, which come into force on January 1, 2020, tighten the norms 17 and 21 of the FSTEC Orders: the requirements for the protection of information contained in information systems and the hardware and software of these systems are defined; established the mandatory requirements for the certification of the information security tools in medical organizations. The servers of such information systems should locate on the territory of the Russian Federation.

Despite significant changes in the field of processing personal data and ensuring information security, there is still a lack of guidelines, and an abundance of documents, often duplicating each other. Prior to the adoption of these acts, medical organizations in the Russian Federation were entitled to choose at their own risk and the allocated funding information security technologies that provide: separate storage of personal information about the patient and genetic data; use of servers and communication channels protected from external threats; authorized access to processed and stored data; data encryption and anonymization; copy protection; creating backup copies of data, etc.

In this regard, it would be possible to assume a sufficient level of protection of the personal data in the Russian Federation if it were not for serious data breaches. For example, two cases of mass leakage were reported in the media in 2019 in the Moscow Region and Lipetsk. So, according to media reports, in the first case, the file server of the ambulance service of the Moscow Region was accessible from the Internet, and there was no user authorization system. An outdated version of the file-sharing protocol was being used. The connected guest could edit and delete files. As a result of such attacks, the number of victims is estimated to be thousands, and in the future, it can be millions. Breach threats are serious, including because of the lack of appropriate sanctions in the Federal Law "On Information…" and the lack of differentiation of liability (controller, data processor).

Along with the existing lacunae and inconsistency of the legislation, it is also necessary to note the excessive discretion of the medical organization in determining rights, and the diffusion of liability among themselves and patients in practice. Representatives of relevant ministries in the Russian Federation noted the vagueness of the wording in the form of informed consent of a patient (access to primary documentation vs. transfer of anonymized data).[2] There are attempts to shift the liability from the medical organization to the sponsor of the genetic research or to exempt the doctor-researcher from the obligation to keep medical privacy, contrary to the provisions of federal law. Often, medical organizations

---

[2] Elena Volskaya. *Protection of personal data of patients participating in scientific and clinical research. Report at a meeting of the Council of public organizations for the protection of patients' rights at the Federal Service for Supervision of Healthcare* (September 18, 2018), http://www.roszdravnadzor.ru/i/upload/images/2018/9/18/1537283104.03682-1-1443.pdf (accessed Dec. 17, 2019).

shift the liability and risks of maintaining privacy to the patient and expand the list of people who can access the patient's primary medical documentation.

Finally, the current legislation of the Russian Federation does not consider the peculiarities of genetic data as object of high commercial value to various economic entities, as well as allowing the identification of other persons. Fixing the status of genetic data as personal and biometric, proposed by the bill of the Government of the Russian Federation, is not enough.[3] The current federal laws do not specifically regulate the issues of obtaining and processing DNA information, informing a person about the progress and results of genetic research, disclosing and protecting the privacy of the data received. The law does not define the right to withdraw informed consent and the procedure for cross-border transfer of genetic data. There is no regulation on permissible disclosure of medical information in special cases (informing relatives, representatives of the patient). The legislator has not resolved the question of the permissibility of a person's open consent to the widespread use of their genetic material, not only for scientific purposes that already provided but also for purposes that may arise in the dynamics of the research process. More detailed regulation in the Russian Federation may need to address the issues of individuals' rights in cases where personal data are processed by data processors. So, it is possible to resolve the issue by sharing the profit of genetic research with individuals who provided their genetic data.

The Russian legislator also needs to take into account international regulatory experience and, in particular, the EU General Data Protection Regulation (GDPR). The Regulation, although providing insufficient protection for the individual[4], provides some

---

[3] Bill № 744029-7 On amendments to Article 11 of the Federal Law "On Personal Data" regarding the processing of biometric personal data (2019)

[4] Selita, F. 2019. Genetic Data Misuse: Risk to Fundamental Human Rights in Developed Economies. *Legal Issues Journal*, 7(1). DOI: doi.org/10.6084/m9.figshare.11423724

new expanded rights and obligations for people who provide data, that have no analogues in Russian legislation. For example, the regulation defines the duty to notify the operator not only the authorities, but also the subject - the carrier of personal data about the case of leakage of such data. The right to data portability between operators, the right to restrict processing, and the right to notify a subject when changing or destroying his personal data provided. The GDPR also determines significant fines for non-compliance with European legislation, independent supervisory authority, and the right of a person to protect his rights effectively.

Overall, two conclusions can be made. First: the use of genetic data in the Russian Federation require special regulation that provides, on the one hand, effective protection of the rights of individuals, and on the other hand, does not create additional restrictions on the conducting of genetic research, including the joint work with foreign organizations. The second conclusion relates to the provisions of Part 2 of Art. 11 of the Federal Law "On Personal Data", expanding the list of cases of processing biometric personal data without the consent of a person for the purposes of the administration of justice and the enforcement of judicial acts, for state defense and countering terrorism, transport security, combating corruption, operational-search activity, public service, and migration. Together with the general genetic identification of the population in the Russian Federation, this regulation will entail changes in the concept of privacy in the Russian Federation.[5] However, is privacy possible in cases where biobanks are State-controlled? Would such practices of the State contradict the provisions of international acts in the field of protection of human rights? In order to answer these questions more public discussion is needed in the Russian Federation.

[5] Ellen W. Clayton, Barbara J Evans, James W Hazel, Mark A Rotstein, *The law of genetic privacy: applications, implications, and limitations*, Journal of Law and the Biosciences Vol 6 Issue 1 (2019).

'Race' and other group discrimination in the genomic era

Fatos Selita[1]

Department of Psychology, Goldsmiths, University of London
Department of Psychology, Tomsk State University

Marc Willers

Garden Court Chambers

Yulia Kovas

Department of Psychology, Goldsmiths, University of London
Department of Psychology, Tomsk State University

Summary. Genetic science has provided new knowledge that has the potential to reduce 'race' discrimination. This includes findings that around 95% of human genetic variability is present within any population; and that most human traits are influenced by a complex combination of many genetic and environmental factors. Despite this knowledge, racially discriminatory practices persist internationally, including segregation; unfair sentencing; state surveillance of children; and

[1] Corresponding author. Email: fatos.selita@gold.ac.uk

involuntary sterilisation. Moreover, there is an emerging risk that DNA may be used to propel harmful discriminatory practices. For example, new 'DNA-based' groups may emerge in the context of polygenic prediction – aggregating multiple genetic risks into individuals' combined risk indexes. Such DNA-based groups could be viewed as 'new races' - adding yet another category to the already heterogenous definition of 'race'. This paper reviews the genetic advances directly relevant to, and their impact on, 'race' and other group discrimination; and assesses current UK and international discrimination practices and effectiveness of the laws in place prior to and in the genomic era. The paper concludes that current laws provide insufficient protection from 'race' and other group discrimination and still reflect people's beliefs in entrenched differences between 'races'. The paper asserts that the very use of the term 'race' in equality legislation is problematic due to inconsistencies in definition across key legislations; and history of its association with domination. Justice systems must update laws to reflect current genetic knowledge and to address existing and emerging risks of discrimination.

Keywords: Discrimination law; race discrimination; genetics and race; DNA based group discrimination; equality legislation; genetics and race

Genetic science has produced a vast amount of knowledge about human traits. This knowledge has the power to bring both great benefits and harm to people. Numerous discrimination practices have been based on the assumed biological / genetic differences among groups – so called 'races'. This paper argues that the risks of such discrimination remain high in the genomic era, which has started in 21st century with the completion of the Human Genome Project (Guttmacher and Collins 2003). The paper highlights the problems with the definition of 'race'. The paper outlines the existing UK law on 'race' discrimination, as well as relevant international instruments, and considers their effectiveness in practice. The paper then highlights how genetic science can be used to minimise race and other group discrimination, but that at the same time may introduce new challenges for justice systems, such as discrimination against *DNA-based* groups. Such groups may, for example, include people who have similar polygenic scores linked to particular traits and/or the same genetic markers for particular conditions. Using an interdisciplinary perspective of law and genetics, the paper identifies what is required from justice systems to update laws to alleviate such risks.

Discrimination on perceived biological differences

History of discrimination

Societies have used heredity for centuries as a predictor of an individual's qualities. Relying on lineage, for example, people have selected partners, employees and social circles. People have long known that something *biological* transmits from generation to generation within families. Today we know that what is transmitted is DNA, the genome. However, our understanding of genetic transmission has been limited, leading to incorrect views about genetic differences between groups and to discrimination of groups. Group discrimination is based on many characteristics, including colour, nationality, ethnicity, religion, class, caste, gender and other existing and perceived differences.

Discrimination based on hypothesised biological differences between groups has led to numerous catastrophes, including the following well known genocides: the murder of up to 1.5 million Armenians in 1915; of around 6 million Jews and hundreds of thousands of Roma in the Second World War; and more recently (1992-95), of around 250,000 Bosnians (genocidewatch.com) (Derderian 2005; Paulsson 2011; ushmm.org n.d.). Other horrific group discrimination practices include, the centuries-long segregation of black people; and the persistent discrimination of minority ethnic groups, such as the Roma people.

Another example of group (class) discrimination is that of eugenic practices that used genetics to support its agenda (Lombardo 1985). The eugenic movement, which originated in England, advocated restricting birth within groups considered genetically inferior, targeting immigrants, minorities and poor people (Andrews, Mehlman, and Rothstein 2015; Bouche and Rivard 2014; Daniel J. Kevles 1985; Kevles 1999; UNICEF 2017). It was erroneously believed that undesirable traits (e.g. feeblemindedness, criminality and alcoholism) were passed on in families in a simple way, and therefore it was thought possible to improve the genetic pool of the population by 'breeding out' disease and intellectual weakness. The father of Eugenics, Francis Galton, proposed that '…as a new race can be obtained in animals and plants, … with moderate care in preventing the more faulty members of the flock from breeding, so a race of gifted men might be obtained… .' ((Galton 1869) p 64). Although Galton did not propose sterilisation to improve race, later millions of people were forcefully sterilised. These forced sterilisations were conducted in the name of 'improving race' and alleviating the 'burden' that the poor, disabled and mentally ill 'impose' on society. Reported numbers of forcefully sterilised people, include around 64000 in the US; 60000 in Sweden; and 3.5 million in Germany (Andrews et al. 2015; Daniel J. Kevles 1985; UNICEF 2017).

In the USA, the Eugenics Records Office (ERO) used unreliable data to promote eugenic practices leading to passing of Eugenic laws. In the most damaging case in the history of Eugenics – *Buck v Bell* 1927 – the US Supreme Court upheld the sterilisation of a poor woman of average intelligence on the ground of 'imbecility', paving the path for millions of sterilisations (Burrus 2016; Georgia State University 1927; Lombardo 1985). For example, 20 states passed eugenic sterilisation statutes in the following 10 years, with the total of 33 US States ennacting sterilisation laws (Andrews et al. 2015; Lombardo 2011; SSHRCC n.d.). The *Buck v. Bell* case has never been overturned.

The eugenic movement spread across the world, and included a number of international organisations and societies which themselves had disagreements on what methods can and should be used to 'improve' a human population (stock) (Macuglia 2014). In the UK, where the first International Eugenics Conference was held in 1912, eugenics was supported by political leaders (Brignell 2010). The UK prime minister, Winston Churchill, for example, is reported to have warned that 'The multiplication of the feeble-minded… is a very terrible danger to the race' (Akomolafe 2016; Larson 2017); and another parliamentarian is reported to have described disabled people as 'human vermin…' (Brignell 2010; Chitty 2009; Sewell 2009).

Using the *inferior race* justification, laws were passed in the USA (e.g. Immigration Act, 1924) to minimise or stop immigrant intakes from a number of nationalities, whose communities were growing large enough to require seats in government (Ager and Hansen 2017; Higham 2002; Ogletree 2000; Stolerman 2017). The set intakes of immigrants were 82% for Northern and Western Europeans; 14% for Southern and Eastern Europeans (e.g. Italians, Slavs and Greeks); and 4% for the rest of the world (Ogletree 2000). This policy/law remained in force throughout the Second World War, at a time when the nationalities allocated small quotas would have had the most need to migrate to the USA.

The use of eugenic laws continued long after the ERO was shut down in 1939 - with the last eugenics laws repealed as late as 1979 in California. Since then, the eugenic laws have been discredited and eugenic practices have been banned worldwide. For example, the Universal Declaration on the Human Genome (1997) states that 'discrimination based on genetic characteristics that is intended to infringe or has the effect of infringing human rights, fundamental freedoms and human dignity' shall be prohibited. In addition, the Universal Declaration of Human Rights (1958) Article 6 states that 'We *should* all have the same level of legal protection whoever we are...'.

However, there are risks that genetic information will continue to be misused. For example, there have been recent reports of eugenic practices continuing, such as sterilisations of inmates reported to have happened as recently as 2010 - 150 women sterilised between 2006-2010 in the State of California (Johnson 2013). Similarly, sterilisations of Roma women are reported to have continued until 2016, for example in Czech Republic (ERRC 2016). Other race discrimination practices based on genetics persist in other advanced economies. For example, Swedish police were found to keep in a secret register details of over 1000 Roma children, some of whom were as young as 2 years old in the form of family trees (Ghosh 2013; Mansel 2013; Reuters 2013). Other alarming trends include the family cap laws in the US – removing financial support for additional children for parents who were already receiving financial assistance (Berkeley Law 2016; Dinkel 2011; Lombardo 2011). These laws spread (in around 25 States in 2011) following the 1996 Personal Responsibility and Work Opportunity Reconciliation Act (PRWORA) which gave States discretion to pass family cap laws (a number of States have now abolished these laws) (Berkeley Law 2016). Family cap laws have been criticised as *punitive restriction to curtail* poorer people's propensity to have more children, which were falsely promoted as 'as a way of minimising reliance on support' and '*solving the intractable' problems of poverty* (Dinkel 2011; Roberts 1997).

Reasons for persistent discrimination

Discrimination on real and perceived genetic differences is a complex multifactorial phenomenon. One reason for persistent discrimination is that historically eugenic laws and propaganda were used to maintain political control – justifying continued suppression of black people, poor people and minority immigrants (Andrews et al. 2015; UNICEF 2017). Commercial agenda can also exharcebate beliefs in racial differences. For example, the BiDil drug, having undersold for decades as a general drug, was rebranded as a solution for a large select 'racial' group (African Americans) – despite research showing no race/ethnic related effect (Bowser 2004; Brody and Hunt 2006; Hammermeister et al. 2009; Husten 2017; Kahn 2004).

Another major factor is that the propensity to discriminate seems to be an inherent feature of the human mind, tightly linked to the propensity to protect one's own group. This seemingly universal human trait is likely to have evolved and is shared with many species. This propensity can often be paradoxical, such as discrimination on grounds of gender which can result in harming closest family members (e.g. mother, sister, wife). In turn, this universal propensity to discriminate creates a fear that someone or some group will necessarily be discriminated. In other words, people discriminate others in order to avoid occupying the 'discriminated niche'. These and other weaknesses might help explain how extreme discrimination and even genocide can occur amongst people of the same nation, such as that which occurred between Hutu and Tutsi people in Rwanda (Epstein 2017).

Discrimination is further exacerbated by people's tendency to readily accept views that support pre-conceived ideas (Gilead, Sela, and Maril 2018). This means that people can easily accept scientifically weak reports and opinions that support their established belief in the existence of racial differences. This tendency is reinforced by another human weakness - the difficulty in correcting fake information that was initially accepted as true, even after learning it was fake (De keersmaecker and Roets 2017). In addition, specific to 'race' discrimination, as discussed in the following section, the very use of the term 'race' in law and legal practice may contribute to the problem.

Law and practice

Problems with the term 'race'

The use of the term 'race' in equality legislation is in itself problematic. It is a term that is 'widely recognised as a social and political construct with a long history, originating in economic and expansionist imperatives and directed as legitimising domination' ((Monaghan 2013) p. 187). Various legislations attempt to distance themselves from accepting the existence of 'race' – demonstrating a somewhat confused position: using the term race and at the same time denying the existence of racial differences. For example, the EU indirectly acknowledges that equality law is based on the misunderstanding of the meaning of the term 'race', and includes the following disclaimer in recital 6 of the EU Directive 2000/43/EC (the 'Race Equality Directive): 'The European Union rejects theories which attempt to determine the existence of separate human races. The use of the term 'racial origin' in this Directive does not imply the acceptance of such theories.' Similarly, Belgian law refers to 'alleged race'; and French law to 'real or assumed race' (European Commission 2016).

The term 'race' is also defined in many ways in domestic legislation and other international instruments, with some including ethnicity, colour, religion, nationality, and other features; some considering 'race' to be a distinct feature in its own right; and others using different characteristics (such as ethnic origin and ethnicity) interchangeably with 'race'. For example:

- In the UK, the Equality Act (EA) 2010 (section 9), defines the term 'race' as encompassing 'colour, nationality, ethnic or national origins'. Under EA 2010, section 9(5), the UK government was required to include 'caste' in the statutory definition of 'race', and in 2014 it was held by a Tribunal that 'caste' does fall within the definition of 'race' (Pyper 2018; UKEAT 2014).
- Article 1 of the International Convention on the Elimination of All Forms of Racial Discrimination 1969 (ICERD) defines racial discrimination to include discrimination on race, colour, descent, or national or ethnic origin.
- Article 14 of the European Convention on Human Rights 1953 (ECHR) states that the enjoyment of the rights to prohibition from discrimination and other rights under the Convention 'shall be secured without discrimination on any ground such as sex, race, colour, language, religion, political or other opinion, national or social origin, association with a national minority, property, birth or other status'.
- The European Commission against Racism and Intolerance (ECRI), a human rights monitoring body, defines 'racial discrimination' to include discrimination on the grounds of 'race, colour, language, religion, nationality or national or ethnic origin' (General Policy Recommendation No. 7).
- The EU's Race Equality Directive states that 'the purpose of this Directive is to lay down a framework for combating discrimination on the grounds of racial or ethnic origin' (Directive 2000/43/EC).
- The Treaty on the Functioning of the EU 2007 (TFEU) states that 'the Union shall aim to combat discrimination based on … racial or ethnic origin…' (Article 10).

These definitions partly overlap with the definition of 'ethnicity' provided by the European Court of Justice (ECJ), which has recently stated that 'ethnicity' has 'its origins in the idea of societal groups marked in particular by common nationality, religious faith, language, cultural and traditional origins and background' (CURIA 2015).

In the UK courts have found that discrimination of an English national by a Scottish employer falls under the definition of 'racial discrimination' – stating that in order to determine whether a group is defined by reference to 'national origins', there must be identifiable historical and geographical elements, separate from the individual's origins, which reveal the existence of a nation at some point in the history of the group (EAT 1997).

Some countries have attempted to formulate anti-discrimination laws without mention of the word 'race'. For example, Germany has focused only on specific grounds of discrimination such a xenophobia and anti-Semitism. However, this approach may lead to the neglect of other forms of discrimination (UN CERD 2017).

Such inconsistent use of the term 'race' in equality legislation may partially stem from the fact that the etymology of the word is not clear and that it has been historically used to mean different things, including: 'people of common descent' from the 16th Century French word 'race'; 'race, breed, lineage, family', from the 16th Century Italian word 'razza'; and English uses varying widely, including, 'group of people with common occupation' (c. 1500), 'generation' (1540s), and 'tribe, nation, or people regarded as of common stock' by 1560s (Online Etymology Dictionary n.d.). However, defining race is not simply a matter of understanding etymology, but rather clarifying a complex issue with implications for human rights of all people. As human rights is a universal issue it makes sense for the definition of what can constitute discrimination to be uniform in domestic jurisdictions across the globe. Overall therefore the issue of the use of the term 'race' has not been resolved and more work is needed to achieve a satisfactory solution.

Effectiveness of legal protection against race discrimination

In the 1960s there was a categorical shift in the UK and the US in the protection of people against 'racial' discrimination when laws were introduced which: prohibited discrimination on grounds of race in public places (segregation), in voting, in housing and other civil rights; and invalidated laws prohibiting interracial marriage (Adams, Bell, and Griffin 2007; Brown 2018).

In the UK, legal protection against 'race' discrimination has gradually been extended and strengthened since the enactment of the first piece of equality legislation in 1965. The law is now encapsulated in the Equality Act (EA) 2010 and can be used to bring discrimination claims against individuals, organisations, private companies and public bodies.

However, there are a number of loopholes in the UK law that allow for 'racial' discrimination. For example, Schedule 3 of the Equality Act 2010 permits the immigration authorities to discriminate on (inter alia) grounds of nationality or ethnic/national origin pursuant to a ministerial authorisation. Indeed, it could be said that the whole system of immigration control is racially discriminatory. The Commonwealth Immigrants Acts 1962 and 1968 were essentially designed for the purpose to deprive certain Citizens of the United Kingdom and Colonies, disproportionately Black and Asian people from overseas colonies/territories, of their previous common law right to live in the UK. The 1968 Act in particular was specifically designed to stop East African Asians settling in the UK. The Immigration Act 1971 replicated those injustices in its concept of 'patriality', which discriminated in favour of Citizen of the UK and colonies (CUKCs) who were born in or had ancestral connections to the UK (disproportionately White British people) and against those who did not. That discrimination was then repeated in the British Nationality Act 1981, which abolished CUKC status and gave the new status of 'British citizen' only to those CUKCs who were patrial.

In 2017 the UN Committee on the Elimination of Racial Discrimination highlighted other loopholes. These include the fact that the UK continues to uphold its restrictive interpretation of the provisions of article 4 of ICERD, which deals with hate crime (hate speech, incitement) – thus allowing greater freedom to the media in relation to racial prejudice than the Convention allows. The UN Committee also found an increase in racial prejudice in the media faced by minority ethnic groups, asylum seekers and immigrants, and lack of effectiveness of the Press Complaints Commission (PCC) (which closed in 2014) in dealing with this issue. For example, the UN Committee raised concerns about the UK government allowing the media to use phrases such as 'illegal asylum seekers' – when in fact it is a contradiction in terms. The UN Committee further criticised the UK for the provisions of the Anti-Terrorism Crime and Security Act 2001, which provides for the indefinite detention without charge or trial, pending deportation, of non-nationals of the United Kingdom who are suspected of terrorism-related activities.

The complexity of the legislative equality provisions and the cost of pursuing discrimination claims are additional barriers that render the law ineffective and inaccessible to most people (Selita 2018; The Lord Chief Justice 2015). The UK has also been singled out (alongside Austria and Luxembourg) by the European Commission for the complexity of discrimination laws which may be deterring victims of discrimination (European Commission 2016).

Moreover, the wide discretion afforded to the judiciary may also contribute to discrimination through allowing conscious and unconscious biases to influence decision making. In fact, an analysis of the UK Ministry of Justice identified judges' discretion as a risk of discrimination in sentencing (The Lammy Review 2017). Several studies have found evidence of such discrimination including in the UK and the US. One large study of over 140,000 cases over 13 years found that, within cities (30 cities covered) in the US, a defendant's sentence could vary by up to 63% depending on the judge (US Sentencing Commission 2019). Statistics show that this discretion contributes to discrimination practices of groups. For example, Black offenders in the US have been found to receive 10% longer sentence than White offenders (Kerby 2012; Nanau et al. In review). Similarly, in the UK Black and Asian defendants have been found to receive considerably longer custodial sentence than White defenders, with Asian defendants receiving the longest sentences (Ministry of Jusice 2017). For example, for all offenders sentenced to immediate custody in 2016, White defendants received an average sentence of around 18 months, and Black and Asian defendants around 24 and 25 months respectively (around 33% higher sentence) (Ministry of Jusice 2017). An investigation conducted by *The Independent* found that between 2009-2017 one in four Black teenage boys convicted of homicide were handed maximum jail sentences (life); and *not one* White teenager was sentenced to more than 10 years (Abu 2018). An independent review found that Black people and other ethnic minorities convicted of a drug offence are around 240% more likely to get a prison sentence than White people (The Lammy Review 2017).

These shortfalls in the law and procedure are among primary reasons for overt / open / institutionalised 'racial' discrimination. There are numerous cases of discrimination that can be described as 'structural racism' (United Nations 2018) and which demonstrate that the legal protection offered by the current laws is insufficient. A striking example is the recent *Windrush Scandal* whereby Black people from former colonies who had arrived in the UK in the 1950s and 60s were, for example, denied health care and other essential services or even deported (Harewood 2018). Some of these people were left without any official record because the government destroyed their disembarkation cards in 2010 (Gentleman 2018).

Other statistics show that group discrimination is also prevalent in areas such as policing and employment. For example, in the UK, use of 'stop and search' powers by the police officers show there is significant discrimination against people from ethnic minorities, with Black people being more than 8 times more likely than others to be stopped and searched (UK Home Office 2019; UN CERD 2017). Gypsies, Roma and Irish Travellers represent only 0.1% of the wider population, they account for 5% of male prisoners (HM Inspectorate of Prisons 2017; Ministry of Jusice 2017). Similarly, Black people make 3% of the population, but make 12% of prisoners, and Black children make 21% of children in custody (e.g. (The Lammy Review 2017)). Statistics also show that Black people and other ethnic minorities are twice as likely as white English to die after the use of force by police officers and the subsequent lack of access to healthcare (United Nations 2018). In relation to employment, between 2010 and 2015, there was a 49% increase in the number of young people (16 to 24 year olds) from ethnic minority backgrounds who were long-term unemployed, whereas there was a 2% decrease among young white people (Equality and Human Rights Commission 2016).

Internationally, in other developed jurisdictions, racial discrimination is similarly prevalent. In Europe, police violence against people from ethnic minorities is reported to happen regularly (Council of Europe 2012). For example, in *Lingurar v Romania* the European Court of Human Rights concluded that four members of a Roma family who had been badly beaten by Romanian police officers during a police raid were the victims of 'institutionalised racism' because 'the decisions to organise the police raid and to use force against the applicants were made on considerations based on the applicants' ethnic origin' (ECtHR 2019). The Court concluded that the authorities automatically connected ethnicity to criminal behaviour. The Court further stated that 'Roma communities are often confronted with institutionalised racism and are prone to excessive use of force by the law-enforcement authorities' (para 80).

In the US, 1 in 9 Black men, aged 28 to 34, are imprisoned, compared with the average of 1 in 30 across the whole male population. Moreover, 1 in 3 Black men can expect to go to prison in their lifetime (Lyons and Pettit 2011; Office of Justice Programs n.d.; The Sentencing Project n.d.). In New York State, in 2017, Black people made up 58% of those being stopped and searched by the police; Latino people made up 32% and White people 9%. 9 out of 10 of those stopped were innocent (e.g. not carrying a weapon); and in fact more White people (1.4%) than Black people (1%) were found to have breached the law (BBC Reality Check team 2018).

Moreover, it was only recently that disturbing racial discrimination took place in health care/medical research. For example, the US National Institute of Health conducted a 40-year long, Tuskegee Syphilis Study, where 399 poor Black people were tricked into the study and, among other things, it was concealed that they had the syphilis virus and they were deprived of treatment (penicillin) - despite the virus being deadly and transmittable to partners and children. Following a leak from the media, the victims of discrimination merely received in apology from the then President, Bill Clinton (1999) (The White House 1997).

Overall therefore, 'racial' discrimination laws are not sufficiently effective, allowing for misconceptions and stereotypes about group differences to feed into practice. For example, if a particular group is viewed as more prone to criminal behaviour, its members are more likely to be stopped by the police, making them more likely to get arrested, and more likely to get convicted than members of other groups. That statistical reality simply reinforces discriminatory attitudes, creating a vicious cycle.

What genetic findings mean for 'race' discrimination

Many misconceptions and stereotypes about group differences are based on assumed genetic differences. In this section we review what modern genetic science tells us about validity of these assumptions.

When considering racial discrimination for the purposes of updating protection or views on differences between populations, it is important to distinguish two different claims that are often wrongly merged together. The first claim is that there are behavioural differences between populations (or so called 'races') such as, for example, in intelligence. The second is that there are genetic differences between populations - hypothesised to underlie the behavioural differences. Both claims are notoriously difficult to test.

First, establishing the existence of group differences is challenging because it is difficult to achieve representative samples – ensuring that the comparison includes the whole range of each groups' representatives in the same proportion. Moreover, the assessment methods must be unbiased. For example, comparing the verbal ability of two groups using the same test would be flawed if one group contained a disproportionate number of non-native language speakers.

Second, having established a particular group difference, it is scientifically extremely challenging to determine the reasons for the observed differences. This is because true experiments with natural groups are not possible: participants cannot be randomised to conditions and extraneous variables cannot be properly controlled. Any observed behavioural differences are likely to result from a large number of underlying factors and processes, including group differences in access to resources, cultural practices, societal pressures, as well as average genetic differences.

A striking example of poor practice in group comparisons is research that claimed differences in intelligence between Black and White people; and the claim that these differences resulted from hereditary factors. Much of such research has been shown to be flawed as it did not control for socio-economic conditions, educational opportunity, testing procedure issues and other extraneous variables (Ioannidis, 2005; Zeggini and Ioannidis, 2009). For example, any observed differences in such studies could arise partly because Black people have been segregated for centuries, limiting access to educational and other resources (see also (Kaplan 2015)). In 2000, the US Department of Health published a report which showed shocking disparities between Black and White Americans, including the infant death rate being more than twice as high for Black Americans, and the heart disease death rate, over 40% higher. Based on the available evidence, the report concluded that there are no known biological or genetic characteristics for these disparities, but rather they were due to complex gene-environmental processes (US HHS 2000).

When any behavioural differences between any groups are convincingly established, these differences can only be interpreted in the context of two phenomena: (1) variation within the groups; and (2) the size of the group difference. For most human traits, variation within any naturally occurring group is wide. For example, an international comparison of school children's performance in different academic disciplines, including students from many countries (80 in 2015 and 2018) demonstrated that performance within each country was widely varied (OECD n.d.). Within one country, the gap in knowledge and skills between the lowest and highest performing students of the same age was equivalent to almost 6 years of schooling (OECD 2012). The same study demonstrated that the average differences between the countries were relatively small, even between the highest and lowest performing countries. This means that in the top performing countries millions of children were performing worse than millions of children in the lowest performing countries.

This point about wide within-group variability is often forgotten when group differences are discussed. *Average* refers to the statistical mean of a given group – a sum of scores from each individual in a group, divided by the number of individuals in the group. Using such statistics, for example, research has shown that females, on average, show greater performance in some aspects of verbal ability than males. In contrast, males consistently outperform females on some aspects of spatial ability, such as navigation or mental rotation of objects (Toivainen et al. 2018). However, these group differences are very small, and the variation within the groups is very wide. Despite this, an erroneous common understanding is that, for example, *every* man (or most men) has somewhat better spatial ability than *every* woman. In reality, millions of women outperform millions of men in spatial ability, and millions of men outperform millions of women in verbal ability. The group statistics tell us nothing about an individual's ability.

The same considerations apply to the hypothesised and established genetic differences between groups, including different populations. The starting point of any discussion of genetic differences between populations or any other real or hypothesised groups is the acknowledgement of ten basic facts about human genetics. First, all humans are related to some extent. Second, all humans are extremely similar genetically, sharing more than 99% of the DNA sequence. Third, the differences that do exist among people stem from millions of locations in the DNA – random variation accumulated in our DNA through DNA copying errors and evolutionary processes. Fourth, this variability is present within all populations and new (de novo) mutations continue to emerge and spread in all populations. Fifth, there are generally no *qualitative* differences among populations, in other words, there are no genetic variants (form/allele of the same gene/genetic marker) that exist in one population that do not or cannot exist in another. In rare cases of discovering region-specific variants, they were present in only 1% of the population (Cheng et al. 2015; Rosenberg et al. 2002). This is also consistent with the finding that all individuals are carriers of a large number (more than 8000) of very rare/de-novo variants – not found in other people (Telenti et al. 2016). Sixth, if any genetic differences across populations do occur, they are *quantitative* – meaning that on average, more people in one population have a particular genetic variant than those in another population.

Seventh, many of the average differences in frequency of occurrence of a particular genetic variant across populations have not been linked to any specific human traits, such as intelligence, personality, educational or occupational outcomes or susceptibility to criminal behaviour. It is possible that some genetic differences do not relate to any meaningful behavioural outcomes. Each human trait is governed by hundreds of genes and thousands of DNA markers (polymorphisms), most of which have not yet been discovered (Plomin and Deary 2015). Like any research field, genetic studies designed to find specific links between genetic variants and variation in traits have limitations, including small effects, limited sample sizes, limited genotyping, and liberal interpretation of results (Ioannidis 2005; Zeggini and Ioannidis 2009). All findings from such studies require multiple replications in independent samples before firm conclusions can be reached.

Eighth, when particular genetic variants are linked to particular traits, they explain individual differences within populations, so that, for example, individuals carrying genetic risks for a particular disorder are more likely to develop the disorder than those who carry an alternative variant of the gene. The same variant may also contribute to the differences in the prevalence of the disorder across populations, if more people in one population are carriers of the risk variant.

Ninth, genetic effects are not deterministic, so that, for example, having a particular risk variant does not mean that one would develop an associated problem. Moreover, a particular variant may represent a risk factor for one trait and a protective factor for another trait – a phenomenon called antagonistic pleiotropy. For example, one mutation linked to blindness was found to have a protective effect for heart disease (Cheng et al. 2015).

Tenth, the same genetic variants can express differently in different environments. This means that removing some societal and economic limitations and pressures may negate negative genetic predispositions. Recent behavioural genetic research has demonstrated that even when people have identical genetic predispositions for certain traits, environmental factors, such as inequality, can enhance or limit these propensities (Selita and Kovas 2018). Most diseases, disorders and other traits result from an interplay of many genetic and environmental factors (Polderman et al. 2015), which we currently do not fully understand (Jing, Su, and Ring 2014; Selita and Kovas 2018). The complex gene-environment processes unravel on physiological, neurological, sociological and psychological levels. Untangling the effects of specific factors is further complicated as they unravel over time and interact with each other. For example, a mother's stress during pregnancy may lead to a cascade of negative genetic expression events for the developing baby, affecting multiple long-term outcomes. Furthermore, environments are responsive to our genetic predispositions. For example, siblings evoke different behaviour from parents and other people, which in turn may affect their development differently.

Findings from population genetics can only be considered in the context of these fundamental facts, as well as in the context of human migration and adaptation. Research has demonstrated average genetic differences between homogenous populations (e.g. (Jiang et al. 2013)) resulting from demographic events, such as migration and relative isolation of populations; genetic processes by which new mutations (genetic variants) occur, recombine, and spread in particular populations; and evolutionary processes, that lead to the spread of most advantageous genetic variants in a particular environment (e.g. dark skin protecting from extreme sun exposure; light skin promoting vitamin D absorption when sunlight is limited). The observed population differences relate to *average* differences in the frequency of occurrence of particular genetic variants/markers or combinations of markers (called haplotypes). These differences have been used for genealogical/ancestry identification, and can be precise, if many markers are examined and very homogeneous groups are considered (Weiss and Long 2009). This is because smaller and more isolated groups are less diverse genetically, through the processes of evolutionary adaptation and interbreeding – making determination of their origin easier. However, as described above, *average* differences mean that a particular genetic variant or haplotype is more likely to occur in a particular population, *not* that it does occur in a particular individual from that select population or that it does *not* occur in a different population.

Research has shown that average genetic differences between populations are small when compared to genetic differences within any population / 'race'. For example, a landmark study of 52 populations showed that within-population differences account for 93 to 95% of the genetic variation; and across population differences, for only 3 to 5% (Rosenberg et al. 2002). Numerous studies have generated similar results (e.g.(Romualdi et al. 2002; Tishkoff and Kidd 2004). These findings suggest that two randomly selected people within one population (e.g. Roma) can be more different genetically than two randomly selected people in two different populations (e.g. Roma and English). In addition, population genetic differences have been mostly established for specific genetic markers and haplotypes, but have not yet systematically investigated the interactive and cumulative effects of many genes (Jiang et al. 2013). This means that any group information may be uninformative in regards to many traits in individuals.

The small genetic differences found among the world populations are geographically continuous (Xing et al. 2009) reflecting migration of populations from their origin, Africa, where the largest genetic variability is to be found (Campbell and Tishkoff 2008; Tishkoff et al. 2009). There is no clear dividing line of populations across the world regions. Although clustering of individuals is correlated with geographic origin, ancestry and even some traditional concepts of 'race', these correlations are imperfect, because genetic variation is distributed in a continuous overlapping way among populations (Jorde and Wooding 2004). Therefore, 'races' cannot be biologically precisely defined (Hunt and Megyesi 2008; Weiss and Long 2009).

For reasons outlined above, in relation to an individual's traits, reliance on any ancestry or perceived 'race' or other group information does not provide the necessary precision. Instead, the direct genetic assessment of an individual is necessary – a fact widely recognised in the growing field of personalised medicine. However, where group information can be and continues to be used today is in the identification of *'at risk groups'* – so that they can be provided with more preventative opportunities (e.g., medical tests and checks). This *'at risk'* information can include information on average frequencies of risk genetic variants in different groups. However, this use will become obsolete when every person's risks can be assessed – a likely possibility as the costs of individual genotyping is becoming very low.

Until such individualised approaches become available to all, extreme caution is needed in relying on group information, for example on health risks or response to treatment – when treating individuals (Chen et al. 2018; Sengupta et al. 2018). Some research suggests the existence of some average differences in the prevalence of some traits (e.g. diseases) across populations, and that these differences may be partly explained by genetic differences (Corona et al. 2013; Han et al. 2017; Wyss et al. 2018). A number of studies examined 'racial' differences in the prevalence of different diseases. For example, one study (not using genomic data) examined risk factors in people with ischemic stroke, and reported that Native Hawaiian, and other Pacific Islanders (NHPI) and Asians were more likely to have diabetes, hypertension, dyslipidemia, and obesity than White people (Nakagawa et al. 2013). Another study reported that American Indians had a higher prevalence of some chronic conditions (Amparo, Farr, and Dietz 2011). However, without caution, applications of such information may bring more harm than good to people from ethnic minority groups (Bowser 2004). Whilst it is true that such information can be used to take preventative measures, it can also be used to discriminate against individuals, for example, through high cost of health insurance.

It has also been claimed that some drugs are more effective in some 'racial' groups than in others. For example, it has been suggested that medications for heart failure are less effective for Black than White people (Campbell and Tishkoff 2008). However, other studies showed that there are 'no clear trial data to show any difference in effect between Black and White patients with heart failure' (Taylor and Ellis 2002). Considering the large genetic diversity within Black people and that these genes would react differently to environments, claims that one drug works better or worse on Black people are misleading. Research has shown that, while there are geographic genetic differences in drug metabolising enzymes, they are of little use because current ethnic labels are insufficient and inaccurate representations of the inferred genetic clusters; and the distribution of drug metabolising enzymes variants differs significantly among these clusters (Wilson et al. 2001).

Taken together, the current scientific understanding of genetics is inconsistent with the concept of 'race'. Therefore, 'racial genetic discrimination' is an oxymoron, a contradiction in terms, because any population is genetically diverse. Paradoxically, the genetic science that has created so much controversy with regard to group discrimination when being highjacked by eugenicists, has generated new knowledge that can be used to combat 'race' discrimination.

However, the same new knowledge has brought new challenges for justice systems. For example, our emerging understanding of which genes are responsible for which human traits, and the advances in genotyping (e.g., whole genome sequencing), enables the creation of *DNA-based groups* – for example composed of people who have similar polygenic scores[2] for particular traits (e.g. personality or medical conditions). These new *DNA-based groups* can be created based on thresholds for particular risks or probabilities. For example, a group may include all individuals who score above a particular cut-off for the *number* of genetic variants associated with aggressive behaviour (or heart disease, mental health issues, etc.). The problem with this approach is that these groupings may be aetiologically as diverse (and therefore misleading) as the concept of 'race'. This is because the same behavioural outcomes (e.g. diseases, abilities) may result from different combinations of genetic and environmental factors. Therefore, two individuals may have the same number (e.g., 10) of genetic risks for a particular trait (e.g., aggressiveness), but considering hundreds of risks may be involved in this behaviour, these two individuals may share no risks in common. The actual probability of developing a trait for an individual is very difficult to estimate because each individual will also have other risk and resilience factors that are not taken into account.

Another way to create DNA-based groups is to aggregate together people with only identical genetic variants for particular traits. This provides more precise distinctions than the current ones, such as ancestry, geographical attributions, or class. Moreover, DNA provides information specific to the time when it is taken: epigenetic markers (e.g., methylation patterns) that are added to the DNA over the course of a person's life can already be used to de-

[2] Recent studies across different domains of life show the importance of the genome in prediction and prevention as applicable to an individual. For example, polygenic risk manifested during primary schooling in lower cognitive abilities, lower self-control, academic difficulties, and truancy, was associated with a life-course-persistent pattern of antisocial behaviour that onsets in childhood and persists into adulthood (Wertz et al. 2018). Many studies show genetic links to health, cognition etc. (e.g. (Trampush et al. 2017)). Polygenic scores found for *years in education* explain some variation in criminal behaviour in adults (2 large-scale studies) e-RISK and Dunedin studies (UK and New Zealand) (Odgers et al. 2012; Poulton, Moffitt, and Silva 2015).

termine one's age, smoking status and health-related traits. In the near future, the use of such sequence-based and methylation-based groupings may become widespread because, individual genetic screening may become easier than socio-demographic profiling, and a more effective way of obtaining information on individuals. In fact, it may never be practical, for example, for insurance companies, police force and other institutions to assess each person's genome and to evaluate genetic and epigenetic processes in the context of each person's circumstances. They may therefore opt for the 'easier and cost-effective solutions', such as placing people with certain combinations of genetic markers under surveillance; tracking in education; or gene-based insurance premiums. These new DNA-based groups are not 'visible' geographically or in terms of physiological features. Indeed, members of the same family may fall within different DNA-based groups. Such DNA-based groups could be viewed as 'new races' - adding yet another category to the already heterogenous definition of 'race'. Updated laws are required to prevent the potential discrimination risks of such approaches.

Overall, advancements in genetic science provide new opportunities for the justice system to combat existing discrimination on the basis of 'race'. However, the genomic era requires that legal professionals have sufficient genetic knowledge to apply genetic findings appropriately and to understand new risks of discrimination. Until our knowledge of complex gene-environment interplay becomes more advanced, we need to exercise caution in interpreting genetic findings, when, for example considering genetic factors in sentencing and other contexts. The dangers of not doing so were recently exemplified by research which has suggested that even erroneously believing that one has a genetic risk can have significant negative psychological and physiological consequences that are greater than any possible effects from the actual gene (Turnwald et al. 2019).

Conclusion and recommendations

Statistics on the prevalence of racial discrimination show that it continues to be a wide-spread phenomenon. Group discrimination has a powerful corrosive impact on societies, affecting not only individuals discriminated, but all people, by virtue of the fact that it harms social cohesion (County Health Rankings and Roadmaps 2015). In the genomic era, the risks of racial discrimination may be increased or reduced, depending on how findings are interpreted and on the five steps listed below.

The existing legal protection in the UK and other countries has been found to be ineffective (e.g (European Commission 2016; UN CERD 2017)). The widespread discrimination that exists in the UK and internationally is underscored by historical myths and outdated genetic concepts. Recent advances in our knowledge on genetic differences within and across populations have not yet been assimilated into the law. Beyond the 'structural racism' the law and education are also ineffective in combatting subtle and covert discrimination, such as discrimination in the recruitment of employees.

The pace at which justice systems have developed over centuries is inconsistent with advances in other areas. We have evolved from primitive societies to exploring space, replacing organs, and even editing our own text of life, the DNA. Human knowledge has been reported to have doubled every century until 1900; every 25 years by the end of the Second World War (Fuller and Kuromiya 1981); and every 13 months or faster today (Schilling 2013). In contrast, the '1000-year evolution' (Courts and Tribunals Judiciary n.d.) of the UK justice system has been slow. In fact, the UK legal profession and justice system have been criticised by leading UK lawyers / legal researchers for having changed little since mid-17th century (Robertson 2006). This criticism applies equally to UK discrimination legislation and practice, which remain somewhat archaic and ineffective.

We propose the UK justice system can reduce discrimination by taking the following five steps (also generally applicable to other legal systems):

1. The terms 'race' and 'racial' discrimination should be removed altogether from equality legislation. The concept of 'race' is not supported by current biological knowledge, but has been linked for centuries with inferiorities and superiorities. Moreover, the term is ambiguous in legal instruments / legislation – presenting barriers to the effectiveness of laws. Reference to 'race' in justice may consciously or unconsciously consolidate this concept in the minds of people, which provides yet another reason for abandoning the term.
2. Instead of using an ambiguous term, legislation should prohibit the discrimination against *identifiable groups*, such as nationality, national origin, skin colour, and possibly a new category – 'DNA-based groups', applied to people sharing specific DNA markers or groups of markers.
3. The legislative exceptions which permit discrimination in areas such as immigration and policing should be removed. Provisions aimed at tackling group hate should be strengthened and the media should be subject to effective regulation.
4. Designing effective legal protection requires sufficient knowledge. Relevant genetic knowledge has been found to be low among advocates and judges, and views on use of genetic information in justice and for crime prevention, very divided (Chapman et al. 2018; Selita, Chapman, and Kovas 2019; Selita et al. In review). The level of knowledge can be raised through short training programmes organised by the judiciary, the Bar Council and the Law Society, as continued professional development for lawyers and judges, especially those working on human rights and

discrimination. Genetic knowledge would also enable lawyers to understand and assess the validity of research – which is very important for justice. As has happened in the recent past, unsupported arguments (bad science) can spread, especially when they support particular agendas (e.g. the suggestion that there are differences in intelligence between 'races'); and when they are in line with established views - which is particularly the case with 'racial' matters.

5. Genetic knowledge has also been found to be low among the general population (Chapman et al. 2018). Increased knowledge in the population can help to combat outdated, discredited and ingrained views on 'race' and help to fight discriminaton. Including updated genetic knowledge in the school curricula, as well as training for a wide range of stakeholders (e.g., teachers, psychologists and the police) is an important step forward. Increased knowledge will also protect people from manipulative and misleading science reporting by the media.

References

Abu, Fedora. 2018. '"Britain Has Long Profiled Black Boys as Criminals, so Is It Any Wonder They Receive Harsher Sentences?"' *The Independent*, July 30.

Adams, Maurianne, Lee Anne Bell, and Pat Griffin, eds. 2007. *Teaching for Diversity and Social Justice*. 2 edition. New York: Routledge.

Ager, Philipp and Casper Worm Hansen. 2017. 'Closing Heaven's Door: Evidence from the 1920s U.S. Immigration Quota Acts'.

Akomolafe, Femi. 2016. *Black Damage*. Lulu.com.

Amparo, Pamela, Sherry L. Farr, and Patricia M. Dietz. 2011. 'Chronic Disease Risk Factors among American Indian/Alaska Native Women of Reproductive Age'. *Preventing Chronic Disease* 8(6):A118.

Andrews, Lori B., Maxwell J. Mehlman, and Mark A. Rothstein Eds. 2015. *Genetics: Ethics, Law and Policy*. 4th Edition. West Academic.

BBC Reality Check team. 2018. 'Do New York Police Unfairly Stop Young Black Men?' September 29.

Berkeley Law. 2016. *Bringing Families out of 'Cap'Tivity: The Path Toward Abolishing Welfare Family Caps*.

Bouche, Teryn and Laura Rivard. 2014. 'America's Hidden History: The Eugenics Movement | Learn Science at Scitable'.

Bowser, Rene. 2004. 'Race as a Proxy for Drug Response: The Dangers and Challenges of Ethnic Drugs'. *DePaul Law Review* 53(3):1111.

Brignell, Victoria. 2010. 'The Eugenics Movement Britain Wants to Forget'. December 9.

Brody, Howard and Linda M. Hunt. 2006. 'BiDil: Assessing a Race-Based Pharmaceutical'. *Annals of Family Medicine* 4(6): 556–60.

Brown, Jennifer. 2018. 'An Early History of British Race Relations Legislation'.

Burrus, Trevor. 2016. 'The United States Once Sterilized Tens of Thousands --Here's How the Supreme Court Allowed It'. January 27.

Campbell, Michael C. and Sarah A. Tishkoff. 2008. 'African Genetic Diversity: Implications for Human Demographic History, Modern Human Origins, and Complex Disease Mapping'. *Annual Review of Genomics and Human Genetics* 9(1):403–33.

Chapman, Robert, Maxim Likhanov, Fatos Selita, Ilya Zakharov, Emily Smith-Woolley, and Yulia Kovas. 2018. 'New Literacy Challenge for the Twenty-First Century: Genetic Knowledge Is Poor Even among Well Educated'. *Journal of Community Genetics*.

Chen, Bifeng, Jingdong Wang, Jieling Wang, Jingli Zhang, Xiuli Gu, and Xianhong Feng. 2018. 'The Study of MDM2 Rs937283 Variant and Cancer Susceptibility in a Central Chinese Population'. *Technology in Cancer Research & Treatment* 17.

Cheng, Ching-Yu, Kenji Yamashiro, Li Jia Chen, Jeeyun Ahn, Lulin Huang, Lvzhen Huang, Chui Ming G. Cheung, Masahiro Miyake, Peter D. Cackett, Ian Y. Yeo, Augustinus Laude, Ranjana Mathur, Junxiong Pang, Kar Seng Sim, Adrian H. Koh, Peng Chen, Shu Yen Lee, Doric Wong, Choi Mun Chan, Boon Kwang Loh, Yaoyao Sun, Sonia Davila, Isao Nakata, Hideo Nakanishi, Yumiko Akagi-Kurashige, Norimoto Gotoh, Akitaka Tsujikawa, Fumihiko Matsuda, Keisuke Mori, Shin Yoneya, Yoichi Sakurada, Hiroyuki Iijima, Tomohiro Iida, Shigeru Honda, Timothy Yuk Yau Lai, Pancy Oi Sin Tam, Haoyu Chen, Shibo Tang, Xiaoyan Ding, Feng Wen, Fang Lu, Xiongze Zhang, Yi Shi, Peiquan Zhao, Bowen Zhao, Jinghong Sang, Bo Gong, Rajkumar Dorajoo, Jian-Min Yuan, Woon-Puay Koh, Rob M. van Dam, Yechiel Friedlander, Ying Lin, Martin L. Hibberd, Jia Nee Foo, Ningli Wang, Chang Hua Wong, Gavin S. Tan, Sang Jun Park, Mayuri Bhargava, Lingam Gopal, Thet Naing, Jiemin Liao, Peng Guan Ong, Paul Mitchell, Peng Zhou, Xuefeng Xie, Jinlong Liang, Junpu Mei, Xin Jin, Seang-Mei Saw, Mineo Ozaki, Takanori Mizoguchi, Yasuo Kurimoto, Se Joon Woo, Hum Chung, Hyeong-Gon Yu, Joo Young Shin, Dong Ho Park, In Taek Kim, Woohyok Chang, Min Sagong, Sang-Joon Lee, Hyun Woong Kim, Ji Eun Lee, Yi Li, Jianjun Liu, Yik Ying Teo, Chew Kiat Heng, Tock Han Lim, Suk-Kyun Yang, Kyuyoung Song, Eranga N. Vithana, Tin Aung, Jin Xin Bei, Yi Xin Zeng, E. Shyong Tai, Xiao Xin Li, Zhenglin Yang, Kyu-Hyung Park, Chi Pui Pang, Nagahisa Yoshimura, Tien Yin Wong, and Chiea Chuen Khor. 2015. 'New Loci and Coding Variants Confer Risk for Age-Related Macular Degeneration in East Asians'. *Nature Communications* 6:6063.

Chitty, Clyde. 2009. *Eugenics, Race and Intelligence in Education*. A&C Black.

Corona, Erik, Rong Chen, Martin Sikora, Alexander A. Morgan, Chirag J. Patel, Aditya Ramesh, Carlos D. Bustamante, and Atul J. Butte. 2013. 'Analysis of the Genetic Basis of Disease in the Context of Worldwide Human Relationships and Migration'. *PLoS Genetics* 9(5).

Council of Europe, ed. 2012. *Human Rights of Roma and Travellers in Europe*. Strasbourg: Council of Europe.

County Health Rankings and Roadmaps. 2015. *2015 Key Findings Report*.

Courts and Tribunals Judiciary. n.d. 'History of the Judiciary'. Retrieved 8 November 2019 (https://www.judiciary.uk/about-the-judiciary/history-of-the-judiciary/).

CURIA. 2015. *CHEZ Razpredeleine Bulgaria AD v Komisia Za Zashtita Ot Discriminatsia.*

Daniel J. Kevles. 1985. *In the Name of Eugenics Genetics and the Uses of Human Heredity*. University of California Press.

De keersmaecker, Jonas and Arne Roets. 2017. '"Fake News": Incorrect, but Hard to Correct. The Role of Cognitive Ability on the Impact of False Information on Social Impressions'. *Intelligence* 65:107–10.

Derderian, Katharine. 2005. 'Common Fate, Different Experience: Gender-Specific Aspects of the Armenian Genocide, 1915-1917'. *Holocaust and Genocide Studies* 19(1):1–25.

Dinkel, Christopher. 2011. 'Welfare Family Caps and the Zero-Grant Situation'. *CORNELL LAW REVIEW* 96:33.

EAT. 1997. *Northern Joint Police Board v Power.*

ECJ. 2015. *CHEZ Razpredelenie Bulgaria AD v Komisia Za Zashtita Ot Diskriminatsia.*

ECtHR. 2019. *Lingurar v. Romania.*

Epstein, Helen C. 2017. 'America's Secret Role in the Rwandan Genocide'. *The Guardian*, September 12.

Equality and Human Rights Commission. 2016. *Healing a Divided Britain.*

ERRC. 2016. *Cohercive and Cruel: Sterilisation and Its Consequences for Romani Women in the Czech Republic (1966-2016).* The European Roma Rights Centre.

European Commission. 2016. *A Comparative Analysis of Non-Discrimination Law in Europe*. Doi:10.2838/080560.

Fuller, R. Buckminster and Kiyoshi Kuromiya. 1981. *Critical Path*. St. Martin's Press.

Galton, Francis. 1869. *Hereditary Genius*. MACMILLAN AND CO. AND NEW YORK.

Gentleman, Amelia. 2018. 'Home Office Destroyed Windrush Landing Cards, Says Ex-Staffer'. *The Guardian*, April 17.

Georgia State University. 1927. *Buck v Bell Documents | Faculty Publications | Georgia State University College of Law.*

Ghosh, Palash. 2013. 'Swedish Police Keep Secret Files On Roma (Gypsy) People: Fighting Crime Or Ethnic Profiling?' *International Business Times*, December 4.

Gilead, Michael, Moran Sela, and Anat Maril. 2018. 'That's My Truth: Evidence for Involuntary Opinion Confirmation'. *Social Psychological and Personality Science* 1948550618762300.

Guttmacher, Alan E. and Francis S. Collins. 2003. 'Welcome to the Genomic Era'. *New England Journal of Medicine* 349(10):996–98.

Hammermeister, Karl E., Diane Fairclough, Caroline Bublitz Emsermann, Richard Hamman, Michael Ho, Stephanie Phibbs, Mary Plomondon, Robert Valuck, David West, and John F. Steiner. 2009. 'Effectiveness of Hydralazine/Isosorbide Dinitrate in Racial/Ethnic Subgroups with Heart Failure'. *Clinical Therapeutics* 31(3):632–43.

Han, Chao, Xi-Kun Han, Fang-Chao Liu, and Jian-Feng Huang. 2017. 'Ethnic Differences in the Association between Angiotensin-Converting Enzyme Gene Insertion/Deletion Polymorphism and Peripheral Vascular Disease: A Meta-Analysis'. *Chronic Diseases and Translational Medicine* 3(4):230–41.

Harewood, David. 2018. 'I'll Fight for the Windrush Generation – Their Treatment Has Been Shameful | David Harewood'. *The Guardian*, April 16.

Higham, John. 2002. *Strangers in the Land: Patterns of American Nativism, 1860-1925*. Rutgers University Press.

HM Inspectorate of Prisons. 2017. *HM Chief Inspector of Prisons for England and Wales: Annual Report 2016–17.*

Hunt, L. M. and M. S. Megyesi. 2008. 'Genes, Race and Research Ethics: Who's Minding the Store?' *Journal of Medical Ethics* 34(6):495–500.

Husten, Larry. 2017. 'Long Unsuccessful Heart Failure Drug Once Again At Center Of Controversy'. *CardioBrief*. Retrieved 3 March 2019 (http://www.cardiobrief.org/2017/01/23/long-unsuccessful-heart-failure-drug-once-again-at-center-of-controversy/).

Ioannidis, John P. A. 2005. 'Why Most Published Research Findings Are False'. *PLoS Medicine* 2(8):e124.

Jiang, Yongshuai, Ruijie Zhang, Hongchao Lv, Jin Li, Miao Wang, Yiman Chang, Wenhua Lv, Xin Sheng, Jingjing Zhang, Panpan Liu, Jiajia Zheng, Miao Shi, and Guiyou Liu. 2013. 'HGPGD: The Human Gene Population Genetic Difference Database'. *PLOS ONE* 8(5):e64150.

Jing, Lijun, Li Su, and Brian Z. Ring. 2014. 'Ethnic Background and Genetic Variation in the Evaluation of Cancer Risk: A Systematic Review'. *PLoS ONE* 9(6).

Johnson, Corey. 2013. 'California Was Sterilizing Its Female Prisoners as Late as 2010 | Corey Johnson'. *The Guardian*, November 8.

Jorde, Lynn B. and Stephen P. Wooding. 2004. 'Genetic Variation, Classification and "Race"'. *Nature Genetics* 36(11 Suppl):S28-33.

Kahn, Jonathan. 2004. 'How a Drug Becomes "Ethnic": Law, Commerce, and the Production of Racial Categories in Medicine'. 4:47.

Kaplan, Jonathan Michael. 2015. 'Race, IQ, and the Search for Statistical Signals Associated with so-Called "X"-Factors: Environments, Racism, and the "Hereditarian Hypothesis"'. *Biology & Philosophy* 30(1):1–17.

Kerby, Sophia. 2012. *The Top 10 Most Startling Facts About People of Color and Criminal Justice in the United States.*

Kevles, Daniel J. 1999. 'Eugenics and Human Rights'. *BMJ: British Medical Journal* 319(7207):435–38.

Larson, Sven R. 2017. *The Rise of Big Government: How Egalitarianism Conquered America*. Routledge.

Lombardo, Paul A. 1985. 'Three Generations, No Imbeciles: New Light on Buck v. Bell'. *New York University Law Review (1950)* 60(1):30–62.

Lombardo, Paul A. 2011. *A Century of Eugenics in America: From the Indiana Experiment to the Human Genome Era*. Indiana University Press.

Lyons, Christopher J. and Becky Pettit. 2011. 'Compounded Disadvantage: Race, Incarceration, and Wage Growth'. *Social Problems* 58(2):257–80.

Macuglia, Daniele. 2014. 'Corrado Gini and the Scientific Basis of Fascist Racism'. *Medicina Nei Secoli* (26(3)):821–855.

Mansel, Tim. 2013. 'Sweden Looks Inward after Roma Revelations'. December 4.

Ministry of Jusice. 2017. *Statistics on Race and the Criminal Justice System 2016.*

Monaghan, Karon. 2013. *Monaghan on Equality Law.* Second Edition, New to this Edition: Oxford, New York: Oxford University Press.

Nakagawa, Kazuma, Matthew A. Koenig, Susan M. Asai, Cherylee W. Chang, and Todd B. Seto. 2013. 'Disparities among Asians and Native Hawaiians and Pacific Islanders with Ischemic Stroke'. *Neurology* 80(9):839–43.

Nanau V, Chapman R, Metzer A, et al. (In review) Computer says 'what?!' Mitigating and aggravating factors in sentencing.

Odgers, Candice L., Avshalom Caspi, Christopher J. Bates, Robert J. Sampson, and Terrie E. Moffitt. 2012. 'Systematic Social Observation of Children's Neighborhoods Using Google Street View: A Reliable and Cost-Effective Method'. *Journal of Child Psychology and Psychiatry, and Allied Disciplines* 53(10): 1009–17.

OECD. 2012. *Key Findings - PISA.*

OECD. n.d. 'About - PISA'. Retrieved 4 March 2019 (http://www.oecd.org/pisa/aboutpisa/).

Office of Justice Programs. n.d. 'Bureau of Justice Statistics (BJS)'. Retrieved 8 November 2019 (https://www.bjs.gov/).

Ogletree, Charles. 2000. 'America's Schizophrenic Immigration Policy: Race, Class, and Reason'. 41:17.

Online Etymology Dictionary. n.d. 'Race | Origin and Meaning of Race by Online Etymology Dictionary'. Retrieved 4 March 2019 (https://www.etymonline.com/word/race).

Paulsson, Steve. 2011. 'BBC - History - World Wars: A View of the Holocaust'. February 17.

Plomin, R. and I. J. Deary. 2015. 'Genetics and Intelligence Differences: Five Special Findings'. *Molecular Psychiatry* 20(1):98–108.

Polderman, Tinca J. C., Beben Benyamin, Christiaan A. de Leeuw, Patrick F. Sullivan, Arjen van Bochoven, Peter M. Visscher, and Danielle Posthuma. 2015. 'Meta-Analysis of the Heritability of Human Traits Based on Fifty Years of Twin Studies'. *Nature Genetics* 47(7):702–9.

Poulton, Richie, Terrie E. Moffitt, and Phil A. Silva. 2015. 'The Dunedin Multidisciplinary Health and Development Study: Overview of the First 40 Years, with an Eye to the Future'. *Social Psychiatry and Psychiatric Epidemiology* 50(5):679–93.

Pyper, Douglas. 2018. 'The Equality Act 2010: Caste Discrimination'.

Reuters. 2013. 'Police Database of Roma Stirs Outrage in Sweden'. *Reuters*, September 23.

Roberts, Dorothy E. 1997. *Killing the Black Body: Race, Reproduction, and the Meaning of Liberty*. Pantheon Books.

Robertson, Geoffrey. 2006. *The Tyrannicide Brief: The Story of the Man Who Sent Charles I to the Scaffold*. Chatto & Windus Vintage.

Romualdi, Chiara, David Balding, Ivane S. Nasidze, Gregory Risch, Myles Robichaux, Stephen T. Sherry, Mark Stoneking, Mark A. Batzer, and Guido Barbujani. 2002. 'Patterns of Human Diversity, within and among Continents, Inferred from Biallelic DNA Polymorphisms'. *Genome Research* 12(4):602–12.

Rosenberg, Noah A., Jonathan K. Pritchard, James L. Weber, Howard M. Cann, Kenneth K. Kidd, Lev A. Zhivotovsky, and Marcus W. Feldman. 2002. 'Genetic Structure of Human Populations'. *Science* 298(5602):2381–85.

Schilling, David Russell. 2013. 'Knowledge Doubling Every 12 Months, Soon to Be Every 12 Hours'. *Industry Tap*, April 19.

Selita, Fatos. 2018. 'Unrepresented Litigants in Modern Courts – Ordeal by Combat'. *Legal Issues Journal* 6(1):35.

Selita, Fatos, Robert Chapman, and Yulia Kovas. 2019. 'To Use or Not to Use: No Consensus on Whether and How to Apply Genetic Information in the Justice System'. *Behavioral Sciences* 9(12):149.

Selita, Fatos and Yulia Kovas. 2018. 'Genes and Gini: What Inequality Means for Heritability'. *Journal of Biosocial Science* 51(1):18–47.

Selita F, V Smereczynska, R Chapman, et al. (In review). Judges on genetics and justice: knowledge, attitudes and opinions.

Sengupta, Debmalya, Udayan Guha, Sagnik Mitra, Sampurna Ghosh, Samsiddhi Bhattacharjee, and Mainak Sengupta. 2018. 'Meta-Analysis of Polymorphic Variants Conferring Genetic Risk to Cervical Cancer in Indian Women Supports CYP1A1 as an Important Associated Locus'. *Asian Pacific Journal of Cancer Prevention: APJCP* 19(8):2071–81.

Sewell, Dennis. 2009. 'How Eugenics Poisoned the Welfare State | The Spectator'. November 25.

SSHRCC. n.d. 'The Eugenics Archives'. Retrieved 8 November 2019 (http://eugenicsarchive.ca/).

Stolerman, Katherine. 2017. 'The American Eugenics Movement: A Study of the Dispersal and Application of Racial Ideologies'. *Aisthesis: Honors Student Journal* 8(2):13–21.

Taylor, Justin S. W. and Gethin R. Ellis. 2002. 'Racial Differences in Responses to Drug Treatment: Implications for Pharmacotherapy of Heart Failure'. *American Journal of Cardiovascular Drugs: Drugs, Devices, and Other Interventions* 2(6):389–99.

Telenti, Amalio, Levi C. T. Pierce, William H. Biggs, Julia di Iulio, Emily H. M. Wong, Martin M. Fabani, Ewen F. Kirkness, Ahmed Moustafa, Naisha Shah, Chao Xie, Suzanne C. Brewerton, Nadeem Bulsara, Chad Garner, Gary Metzker, Efren Sandoval, Brad A. Perkins, Franz J. Och, Yaron Turpaz, and J. Craig Venter. 2016. 'Deep Sequencing of 10,000 Human Genomes'. *Proceedings of the National Academy of Sciences of the United States of America* 113(42):11901–6.

The Lammy Review. 2017. *The Lammy Review: An Independent Review into the Treatment of, and Outcomes for, Black, Asian and Minority Ethnic Individuals in the Criminal Justice System.*

The Lord Chief Justice. 2015. *The Lord Chief Justice's Report 2015*. Judiciary of England and Wales.

The Sentencing Project. n.d. 'Criminal Justice Facts'. *The Sentencing Project.* Retrieved 16 May 2019 (https://www.sentencingproject.org/criminal-justice-facts/).

The White House. 1997. 'Tuskegee Study - Presidential Apology'. Retrieved 8 September 2019 (https://www.cdc.gov/tuskegee/clintonp.htm).

Tishkoff, Sarah A. and Kenneth K. Kidd. 2004. 'Implications of Biogeography of Human Populations for "race" and Medicine'. *Nature Genetics* 36(11s):S21.

Tishkoff, Sarah A., Floyd A. Reed, Françoise R. Friedlaender, Christopher Ehret, Alessia Ranciaro, Alain Froment, Jibril B. Hirbo, Agnes A. Awomoyi, Jean-Marie Bodo, Ogobara Doumbo, Muntaser Ibrahim, Abdalla T. Juma, Maritha J. Kotze, Godfrey Lema, Jason H. Moore, Holly Mortensen, Thomas B. Nyambo, Sabah A. Omar, Kweli Powell, Gideon S. Pretorius, Michael W. Smith, Mahamadou A. Thera, Charles Wambebe, James L. Weber, and Scott M. Williams. 2009. 'The Genetic Structure and History of Africans and African Americans'. *Science (New York, N.Y.)* 324(5930):1035–44.

Toivainen, Teemu, Giulia Pannini, Kostas A. Papageorgiou, Margherita Malanchini, Kaili Rimfeld, Nicholas Shakeshaft, and Yulia Kovas. 2018. 'Prenatal Testosterone Does Not Explain Sex Differences in Spatial Ability'. *Scientific Reports* 8(1):13653.

Trampush, J. W., M. L. Z. Yang, J. Yu, E. Knowles, G. Davies, D. C. Liewald, J. M. Starr, S. Djurovic, I. Melle, K. Sundet, A. Christoforou, I. Reinvang, P. DeRosse, A. J. Lundervold, V. M. Steen, T. Espeseth, K. Räikkönen, E. Widen, A. Palotie, J. G. Eriksson, I. Giegling, B. Konte, P. Roussos, S. Giakoumaki, K. E. Burdick, A. Payton, W. Ollier, M. Horan, O. Chiba-Falek, D. K. Attix, A. C. Need, E. T. Cirulli, A. N. Voineskos, N. C. Stefanis, D. Avramopoulos, A. Hatzimanolis, D. E. Arking, N. Smyrnis, R. M. Bilder, N. A. Freimer, T. D. Cannon, E. London, R. A. Poldrack, F. W. Sabb, E. Congdon, E. D. Conley, M. A. Scult, D. Dickinson, R. E. Straub, G. Donohoe, D. Morris, A. Corvin, M. Gill, A. R. Hariri, D. R. Weinberger, N. Pendleton, P. Bitsios, D. Rujescu, J. Lahti, S. Le Hellard, M. C. Keller, O. A. Andreassen, I. J. Deary, D. C. Glahn, A. K. Malhotra, and T. Lencz. 2017. 'GWAS Meta-Analysis Reveals Novel Loci and Genetic Correlates for General Cognitive Function: A Report from the COGENT Consortium'. *Molecular Psychiatry* 22(3):336–45.

Turnwald, Bradley P., J. Parker Goyer, Danielle Z. Boles, Amy Silder, Scott L. Delp, and Alia J. Crum. 2019. 'Learning One's Genetic Risk Changes Physiology Independent of Actual Genetic Risk'. *Nature Human Behaviour* 3(1):48.

UK Home Office. 2019. *Stop and Search.*

UKEAT. 2014. *Chandhok & Anor v Tirkey.*

UN CERD. 2017. *Protection Against Racial Discrimination in the EU.* United Nations OHCHR.

UNICEF. 2017. *Eugenics.* https://www.history.com/topics/germany/eugenics. Last accessed, 6 Sep 2019.

United Nations. 2018. 'UN Human Rights Experts Says Deaths in Custody Reinforce Concerns about "Structural Racism" in UK'. Retrieved 8 September 2019 (https://www.ohchr.org/en/NewsEvents/Pages/DisplayNews.aspx?NewsID=22997&LangID=E).

US HHS. 2000. *Health People 2010: Understanding & Improving Health.* Washington, D.C.: U.S. Dept. of Health and Human Services.

US Sentencing Commission. 2019. *Intra-City Differences In Federal Sentencing Practices: Federal District Judges in 30 Cities, 2005 - 2017.*

ushmm.org. n.d. 'Documenting Numbers of Victims of the Holocaust and Nazi Persecution'. Retrieved 1 March 2019 (https://encyclopedia.ushmm.org/content/en/article/documenting-numbers-of-victims-of-the-holocaust-and-nazi-persecution).

Weiss, Kenneth M. and Jeffrey C. Long. 2009. 'Non-Darwinian Estimation: My Ancestors, My Genes' Ancestors'. *Genome Research* 19(5):703–10.

Wertz, J., A. Caspi, D. W. Belsky, A. L. Beckley, L. Arseneault, J. C. Barnes, D. L. Corcoran, S. Hogan, R. M. Houts, N. Morgan, C. L. Odgers, J. A. Prinz, K. Sugden, B. S. Williams, R. Poulton, and T. E. Moffitt. 2018. 'Genetics and Crime: Integrating New Genomic Discoveries Into Psychological Research About Antisocial Behavior'. *Psychological Science* 29(5):791–803.

Wilson, J. F., M. E. Weale, A. C. Smith, F. Gratrix, B. Fletcher, M. G. Thomas, N. Bradman, and D. B. Goldstein. 2001. 'Population Genetic Structure of Variable Drug Response'. *Nature Genetics* 29(3):265–69.

Wyss, Annah B., Tamar Sofer, Mi Kyeong Lee, Natalie Terzikhan, Jennifer N. Nguyen, Lies Lahousse, Jeanne C. Latourelle, Albert Vernon Smith, Traci M. Bartz, Mary F. Feitosa, Wei Gao, Tarunveer S. Ahluwalia, Wenbo Tang, Christopher Oldmeadow, Qing Duan, Kim de Jong, Mary K. Wojczynski, Xin-Qun Wang, Raymond Noordam, Fernando Pires Hartwig, Victoria E. Jackson, Tianyuan Wang, Ma'en Obeidat, Brian D. Hobbs, Tianxiao Huan, Hongsheng Gui, Margaret M. Parker, Donglei Hu, Lauren S. Mogil, Gleb Kichaev, Jianping Jin, Mariaelisa Graff, Tamara B. Harris, Ravi Kalhan, Susan R. Heckbert, Lavinia Paternoster, Kristin M. Burkart, Yongmei Liu, Elizabeth G. Holliday, James G. Wilson, Judith M. Vonk, Jason L. Sanders, R. Graham Barr, Renée de Mutsert, Ana Maria Baptista Menezes, Hieab H. H. Adams, Maarten van den Berge, Roby Joehanes, Albert M. Levin, Jennifer Liberto, Lenore J. Launer, Alanna C. Morrison, Colleen M. Sitlani, Juan C. Celedón, Stephen B. Kritchevsky, Rodney J. Scott, Kaare Christensen, Jerome I. Rotter, Tobias N. Bonten, Fernando César Wehrmeister, Yohan Bossé, Shujie Xiao, Sam Oh, Nora Franceschini, Jennifer A. Brody, Robert C. Kaplan, Kurt Lohman, Mark McEvoy, Michael A. Province, Frits R. Rosendaal, Kent D. Taylor, David C. Nickle, L. Keoki Williams, Esteban G. Burchard, Heather E. Wheeler, Don D. Sin, Vilmundur Gudnason, Kari E. North, Myriam Fornage, Bruce M. Psaty, Richard H. Myers, George O'Connor, Torben Hansen, Cathy C. Laurie, Patricia A. Cassano, Joohon Sung, Woo Jin Kim, John R. Attia, Leslie Lange, H. Marike Boezen, Bharat Thyagarajan, Stephen S. Rich, Dennis O. Mook-Kanamori, Bernardo Lessa Horta, André G. Uitterlinden, Hae Kyung Im, Michael H. Cho, Guy G. Brusselle, Sina A. Gharib, Josée Dupuis, Ani Manichaikul, and Stephanie J. London. 2018. 'Multiethnic Meta-Analysis Identifies Ancestry-Specific and Cross-Ancestry Loci for Pulmonary Function'. *Nature Communications* 9(1):2976.

Xing, Jinchuan, W. Scott Watkins, David J. Witherspoon, Yuhua Zhang, Stephen L. Guthery, Rangaswamy Thara, Bryan J. Mowry, Kazima Bulayeva, Robert B. Weiss, and Lynn B. Jorde.

2009. ‘Fine-Scaled Human Genetic Structure Revealed by SNP Microarrays’. *Genome Research* 19(5):815–25.

Zeggini, Eleftheria and John P. A. Ioannidis. 2009. ‘Meta-Analysis in Genome-Wide Association Studies’. *Pharmacogenomics* 10(2):191–201.

Public danger of unauthorized use of human genetic data

Dmitriy Karelin [1]

Law Institute, Tomsk State University

Summary. Scientific and technological progress, the development of technologies, the consistent accumulation of empirical material on human genetic data and their potential value will objectively expand the conditions for their both legitimate and unlawful use. Therefore, the question of legal protection of human genetic data may arise in the very near future.

What legal means can protect human genetic data from misuse?

The protection of the object of encroachment depends on the dynamics of public danger from acts and can be carried out by various legal means (civil, administrative, criminal law). But, in any case, the protection of new social relations begins with the definition of social value, the significance for society of what needs to be protected. Can society do without what the act encroaches on?

---

[1] Corresponding author. Email: karelin@inbox.ru

The issue of the legal nature of human genetic data has already become controversial (Selita,[2] Rothstein,[3] Karelin[4]). It should be agreed that human genetic data are included in the content of human rights and can be attributed to fourth-generation human rights. One of the types of such rights is somatic rights, which (translated from the Greek "soma - body") have a complex legal nature (personally materialistic and personalizing).

In the current system of legal regulation in Russia, genetic data, as relating to an individual person, relating only to this person and being biometric personal data, legally fit into the design of the "right to privacy". Therefore, genetic information about a person can and should be kept secret, and their confidentiality should be considered in the context of the right to respect for human dignity.

The issue of the limits of "secrecy" (confidentiality) of a person's personal data in modern society should be decided considering the balance of interests of the individual, society and the state. This complex issue requires further study.

The legal regulation of relations in the field of the handling of human genetic data should not create obstacles to their legitimate use; and should not create "niches" and conditions for possible abuse by both competent state bodies and other participants in dealing with such data (commercial organizations, medical institutions, private individuals).

Minimizing the above risks is possible. Their identification can be facilitated by the criminological examination of both existing and draft (developed) regulatory legal acts in the field of handling

---

[2] Andrews, L.B., Mehlman, M.J., Rothstein, M.A., 2015. Genetics: Ethics, Law and Policy, 4th Edition. ed. West Academic.

[3] Karelin, D. V., Matsepuro, D. M., Selita, F., 2018. Criminal Legal Protection of Genetic Data of The Person: to Statement of a Problem. *Putnik Journal*. https://doi.org/10.17223/22253513/29/7

[4] Selita, F. 2019. Genetic Data Misuse: Risk to Fundamental Human Rights in Developed Economies. *Legal Issues Journal*, 7(1). DOI: doi.org/10.6084/m9.figshare.11423724

human genetic data. Criminological expertise will identify bottlenecks, predict and evaluate both the favorable and negative consequences of legal regulation.

After determining the social value and significance of what should be protected by legal measures, it is important to determine: in what way can the "damage" of protected good (legal good, legal interest) be expressed? In other words, it is necessary to determine how the object of protection can be destroyed or damaged (physically); and whether the established order/schedule of possession and use of this object can be violated. Applied to human genetic data, it is possible to destroy the biological material itself, from which the genetic information has been extracted; and to destroy, damage and modify this information (or the material information carrier); the established procedure for using (trafficking) this data may be violated; and unauthorized access and unlawful use of human genetic data may occur (for example, hacking a database, copying and subsequent storage, alienation, dissemination of information).

Obviously, human genetic data (both information on a material or other medium) and biological material can be "damaged" through negligence as a result of failure to take measures to preserve them, violation of the rules handling them, etc. This is relevant, for instance, in the process of exchanging databases (biobank) both nationally and internationally. Therefore, of great importance are the development of legal mechanisms for the protection of genetic data and the selection of the type of legal measures are legal consolidation of the respective duties of the person, and the real possibility of their fulfillment. The above circumstances will affect the form and method of committing the offense, as well as the consolidation of a specific form of guilt (intent or negligence) in relation to the act committed by a person.

Understanding the nature and degree of public danger of the unlawful use of human genetic data does not at all mean the unconditional and immediate criminalization of these acts, that is, their recognition in criminal law as criminal and criminally punishable. Legislative consolidation should be preceded by a process assessing the need and expediency of such criminalization, the possibilities of the criminal justice system, the protective potential of other branches of law (civil, administrative), the possibility of using administrative prejudice, and other conditions for criminalizing acts. One of the important conditions for criminalization is to consider the requirements of international legal acts, which in the current legal regulation system have priority over domestic law (part 4 of article 15 of the Constitution of the Russian Federation).

The choice of remedies and the possible criminalization of the misuse of human genetic data will also depend on the prevalence of such acts - an optional sign of public danger.

The effectiveness of protecting human genetic data from socially dangerous encroachments will largely depend on the development and implementation of uniform legal mechanisms, standards for their legitimate use, on the unification and universalization of the conceptual apparatus in this area. Cross-disciplinary and comparative studies will contribute to this.

Justice in the genomic and digital era: a 'different world' requiring 'different law'

Fatos Selita[1]

Department of Psychology, Goldsmiths, University of London

Department of Psychology, Tomsk State University

Summary. Discoveries in the last two decades have created a 'different world', which requires 'different' laws. They have created a world where: enormous information on people's past, present and future can be extracted from DNA alone; the DNA of millions of people has already been sequenced; the cost of sequencing is around 30 million times less than in 2003; additional detailed personal information is collected from numerous sources, such as mobile phones, hospitals, bank cards; this information is shared internationally among numerous powerful private and State organisations; and use of this information can be highly profitable for these organisations. Under these conditions, current law is unable to fully protect rights such as that of *data protection*, *privacy*, *a fair trial*, and *non-dis-*

[1] Corresponding author. Email: fatos.selita@gold.ac.uk.

crimination on genetics and other basis – rights valued by societies. For the law to serve its key purpose, it now must adapt (evolve) to this fast and fundamental change in the 'environment'. In relation to protection from data misuses, as privacy (genetic and other) is not possible, laws are required which can minimise negative impact of data misuses. Key stakeholders (e.g. judges, policymakers) would need to understand how genes work and how genetic information is used in order to appreciate the urgency of updating laws and to build effective protection.

Keywords: genetic privacy, genetic discrimination, digital era, genomic laws, genetic data protection, genetic risks, genetics and justice.

The 'different world' requiring adaptation of the law

Justice systems in advanced economies, such as the UK, EU, US and Canada, pride on 'providing' *a fair trial, data protection* and *privacy*, and *non-discrimination on genetics and other grounds*. The right to a fair trial, privacy and data are fundamental rights in these countries. Similarly, the right to equal treatment – non-discrimination, including protection from genetic discrimination – is a well-established right in the law.

However, the categorical shifts in knowledge – such as the ability to peer into our text of life (DNA) for information on behaviour – has created a fundamentally different environment for the law. The change means the law cannot ensure justice, unless the law evolves to be suitable for the new environment. There are a number of reasons why a fundamental evolution of the law is required, five of which are identified below.

1. People's data, rich with information on the past, present and the future are shared among numerous private and State bodies internationally.

Data are now collected from numerous sources: hospitals, bank cards, mobile phones, shopping and gym memberships, online media, phone calls, emails, state managed CCTVs, AI Google and other technologies. These data are sufficient to build a clear picture on individuals (Executive Office of the President, 2014), and when combined with genetic data – they provide a powerful source for prediction of future behaviour and traits.

It is now indisputable that genetic data provide in-depth information across virtually all human traits such as health, education performance, downward or upward mobility on the social ladder, intelligence and aggressiveness (e.g. (Belsky et al., 2018; Plomin et al., 2016; Polderman et al., 2015). The information we can extract from genetic data alone is continuously growing for a number of reasons: genetic and technological sciences are progressing fast; larger datasets are available; and genetic data are cross-analysed with other available data, including medical and lifestyle data. Larger samples are enabled due to sequencing costs being incomparably smaller (over 30 million times) than when the first human genomes were sequenced.

There are numerous discrimination and other threats to people stemming from genetic research, with limited protection provided by the law (e.g. (Andrews et al., 2015; Furrow et al., 2013; Selita, 2019b). Threats include discrimination in regard to: access to insurance (e.g. health, disability, long-term care, life); access to employment; access to education and educational funding; access to benefits of genetics; and state surveillance. The information on predicted risks extracted from DNA and other data available is also likely to be used to form groups composed of people falling within certain risk thresholds (e.g. using polygenic scoring) – creating DNA-based groupings / new 'races' that can be discriminated

(Selita, et al., 2020). Groups are likely be formed as to specific traits (e.g. risk of mental health, or intelligence), and all traits combined. Other risks include influencing decisions such as voting and career path; and harm to children's rights as children have no say on whether their genome is sequenced.

A more recent but growing threat is to consumers. Consumers are already being misled into buying products which, for example, claim to enhance or suppress genetic expression; and which may be harmful. For example, products and interventions which claim to 'clean' your genes from the 'dirt' they gain during life, e.g. through smoking, have been advertised (Lynch, 2018; The Jakarta Post, n.d.). Direct to consumer testing results are generally provided for only a few locations in the DNA, leading to misinformation on risks. These are likely to cause psychological, financial and other harms to people (Turnwald et al., 2019).

Furthermore, States are also likely to have an interest in interstate genetic data sharing for several purposes, such as crime, immigration and border control. For example, genetic data are likely to be used in immigration, such as when determining visa applications, or application to extend stay or remain. In the US, under a new policy, now being challenged in the US courts, the border agency is to assess any risk of a person being a burden, including health risks, in determining whether a person is given a visa to the US, an extension of stay or a right to remain (Federal Register, 2018; *Cook Cnty. V. McAleenan*, n.d.; [USC02] 8 USC 1182: Inadmissible aliens, 2019). In such cases, data banks which include genetic information provide probabilistic prediction, and so are highly likely to be used.

2. Data are processed in large data banks by multiple parties across the world, and are accessible from anywhere with an internet connection and password – making data highly vulnerable to breaches.

Technological advances have made possible that we process data in a way which allows tailored access to researchers – to as much data as they need and can pay for. However, this means that anyone with similar digital access information, can access the data. This allows for large-scale data breaches from anywhere on the planet (with an internet connection). This is evident from the number of reported large-scale data breaches, which reaches billions per year (e.g. 1,378,509,261 in 2016 alone (Cyentia Institute, 2016)). Moreover, breaches are large scale, for example the reported average size of data breaches for 2019 was 25,575 records (Ponemon Institute, 2019).

Moreover, this multi-national multi-party processing makes enforcement by people practically impossible. This is because it is difficult to assess the jurisdiction of breach; which party breached the data (e.g. whether they happened due to a hack, a system glitch, or an intentional breach); and which part of data were breached. In addition, data protection laws are vague and with numerous loopholes, and conflict with laws that forbid hindrances to data sharing; computing laws are undeveloped; damages are difficult to calculate; and expert involvement in all areas concerned are required, exacerbating the already high costs of court action (e.g. see (Moorhead et al., 2005; Selita, 2018, 2019b)).

3. Data are fused - processed in data-banks combining genetic, phenotypic, medical and other data – making it difficult to determine from which type data the harm resulted.

Data fusion makes it difficult to assess whether discrimination resulted from use of, for example, medical data, genetic data, lifestyle data, or from analysis of all of these data combined. This allows for discriminatory outcomes which are based on forbidden use of data (e.g. genetic data for health insurance determination), to be 'hidden' claiming that information was obtained from data which are allowed (e.g. medical data for insurance determination). Similarly, discrimination (e.g. in surveillance by enforcement agencies) could be excused on the basis of information obtained from data available online from some unknown breach.

The data would also have generally originated from different sources, such health care providers, mobile phone companies, research institutions, enforcement agencies. This makes difficult determining the source of data, and therefore award damages to the injured party. For example, discrimination could have resulted from data sourced from mobile phone companies, from hospitals, from genotyping companies, or from geno-pheno banks. For practical purposes, therefore, data fusion means that data-related rights become only theoretical.

Regardless of this negative outcome, the data fusion of genetic and other data will grow – primarily because it enables reaching the goal of processing, such as predicting and influencing behaviour, and better understanding of the aetiology of traits. The human genome and its functioning are highly complex and vary for each individual. For example, DNA of each new person has been found to contain over 8000 mutations not seen in other sequenced genomes (Telenti et al., 2016). Moreover, genes expressing differently in different environments, makes understanding of aetiology of traits also largely reliant on cross-analyses of genetic data with other big data.

4. The large value of data, now being the new 'gold mines' and seen as exploitable raw material – has led to a strong interest in data collecting, analysing and sharing, as well as numerous large-scale data breaches.

Data now account for a significant amount of the GDP of advanced economies (e.g. around 4 percent for the EU) (EC Data Policy and Innovation, 2018). Moreover, data are valuable in many industries, including advertising, scientific research, market research, voting, and development of drugs. States have also shown a strong interest in using various data for crime prediction and immigration control (Hao, 2019; The Law Society, 2019). Genes accounting for around 50% of differences in traits – means that genetic data are highly informative for prediction, including of criminal behaviour. Surveillance on genetic prediction would decrease surveillance costs (continuously assessing video surveillance is likely to be more costly) and may be more precise, especially when genetic data are analysed in combination with other big data. Moreover, States would have an interest in using predictive information for immigration and border control, to grant visas and stay to only people who are likely to only bring benefits to the economy.

The unique features of genetic data make them also useful for determining criminal liability. The use of genetic information in court is growing in a number of countries (de Kogel & Westgeest, 2015; Farahany, 2015), and is likely to expand further with developments of AI.

5. A key pride of law is the undertaking to provide a fair trial to all people, but findings on human traits and behaviour, including 'free' will, show that under the current law that is not possible.

Law is based on incorrect long-held beliefs that (beyond insanity) people have equal control over their behaviour (free will), that they choose what they do, and that therefore they must be held accountable for their action; and a wide discretion is left to decision-makers (Nanau et al., In review). Research shows that will is like any other trait, and therefore similar in origin and variability – namely, a product of complex gene and environment processes; and of enormous variability, similar to that of intelligence, motivation and schooling (Malanchini et al., 2017; OECD, 2012).

The law therefore cannot provide a fair trial with one-size-fits-all system, and especially one that is not designed for the general public, but only for trained lawyers (The Lord Chief Justice, 2015). Neither can the law issue fair sentence though using incorrect basis of origin of behaviour or control over it, and allowing for individual judges to decide using own discretion, it also inevitably having a wide variability – for example, 63 % variability among judges within cities in sentence issued for same offence with similar circumstances (US Sentencing Commission, 2019).

Other key considerations

Several additional interconnected factors undermine protection of people's rights in the genomic era.

The powerful parties such as corporations and State organisations have capacity to discriminate using sophisticated data processing; and the benefits of data breaches outweigh the related risks. The current laws generally tilt heavily in favour of large players. This is evident from a number of past and recent breaches, such as that of the Tuskegee Syphilis Study; and that of GlaxoSmithKline (GSK) recently. Tuskegee Syphilis Study of the US National Institute of Health, which lasted for 40 years, tricked black people into joining the study by lying to them; concealed information on whether they had the virus; and withheld medication when it became easily accessible (penicillin) – despite the virus being deadly and transmittable through sexual intercourse and congenially (The White House, 1997). The outcome was that the victims received an apology from the US president, and no one faced criminal liability. Similarly, but at a greater scale, GSK admitted criminal liability to numerous serious crimes in the US, including to selling for many years unproved drugs which for example increased suicide thought on teenagers; faking research results; and bribing doctors to prescribe these drugs (GSK) (*United States v. GlaxoSmithKline*, 2012). Yet, no individual faced criminal liability. These examples show that people's rights related to misuse of data are not protected.

The line is blurry between the State, which is to arrange for the protecting of people, and private corporations, which have commercial interests as a primary motivation. This is evident from that fact that large private corporations are often a key part of the process in election of governments and are seen by governments as 'too big to fail'. This interferes with passing of effective laws and actions against corporations. For example, following the serious crimes committed and admitted by GSK (above), which affected large numbers of people – the result was not *decision against*, but an *agreement with*, and no individual facing criminal liability. In contrast, a shoplifting by an individual, when the shoplifting is of a low value, could lead to imprisonment of up to 6 months by Magistrates (Sentencing Council, n.d.).

The enforcement is limited even for straight-forward *fundamental* rights. Examples include, there being no clarity in the law for use of children's heel prick blood samples (Arnold, 2013; Bearder v. Minnesota State 2011); or for access to personal data that are being processed by a public and private body (subject access request). This is primarily because the law allows for numerous exceptions when these rights will not be available; the process of enforcement is highly lengthy and complicated; and the law is not clear, presenting risks for litigation costs of both sides.

Despite many uncertainties in regards to the use of genetic information in the justice system, research shows that the majority of key stakeholders (e.g. judiciary and lawyers) endorse use of genetic data by the State for crime prevention (Selita, et al., In Review; Selita, et al., 2020). The situation is further worsened by the fact that legal professions are generally not representative of societies (e.g. in England and Wales) – with a disconnect in, for example, values and experiences – affecting representation and judgement outcomes (Selita, 2019a).

Conclusion: what next for justice systems?

Overall, the law cannot sufficiently protect the well-established fundamental rights affected by misuses of personal data, such as discrimination and privacy. Having non-enforceable laws is similar to having non-effective medication, but the 'placebo' effect is unlikely to apply in cases where laws make strong promises for protection of highly valued rights such as that of data and privacy. Some solution to protecting people from misuse of data in the current era needs to be found. A large number of people are negatively affected and to be affected, with implication for all people (County Health Rankings and Roadmaps, 2015). There is a likely growing tension within societies, further harming social cohesion, which is already at high risk (e.g. due to high inequality (Selita & Kovas, 2018).

Data-based (genetic and other) discrimination, will affect those at higher risk and their families, which means millions of people. Millions of genomes have already been sequenced despite sequencing being expensive. The first sequencing which was completed in 2003 cost over 30 million times more than today (10,000 researchers, over 10 years and 2.7 billion USD vs. 40 minutes and 399 USD (Dante Labs, n.d.; Goyal et al., 2017)) – soon therefore sequencing will become common. Only a small proportion that have low risks (e.g. health, aggressiveness), would not be negatively affected.

The law will therefore need to: either follow what societies value (e.g. protect people's privacy or from harm caused from lack of privacy); or make people follow the law as it is (e.g. make clear to people that there are no such rights, e.g. privacy, data protection, protection from genetic discrimination).

One option is to focus on making provisions that would render genetic information unusable for harm. For example, instead of preventing insurers from using genetic data, provision of health, disability and life insurance should be regulated by the State, making it accessible to all. This could, for example, be done using similar models to those of Netherlands and Switzerland. This would also save the industry, which is otherwise unlikely to survive the genomic era. Where possible, merely theoretical access to provisions (rights) should be avoided. For example, healthcare in the UK, being funded mostly through general taxation, is free to access. However, based on numerous examples, access is made difficult though numerous hurdles. These include long waits, very limited availability of doctors (e.g. two fixed slots in three months), and unwelcoming treatment (through insurance, one can generally get seen within a week, and receive an outstanding service).

A number of other recommendations specific to the genomic era have been put forward in previous research (Chapman et al., 2018; Karelin et al., 2018; Nanau et al., In review; Selita, 2019b; Selita, et al., In review). These include, creating interdisciplinary working groups to work on updating law and policy in the area; consolidating laws rather than adding new legislation to the already immense pool of laws (Law Commission, 2018); training of key stakeholders such as judiciary as part of professional development, and members of *Committees / Working Groups* allocated the task of overseeing the need for legal updates in this area, such as the House of Lords Science and Technology Committee (Parliament.uk, n.d.); and inclusion of training on genetics in the legal training and other curricula. Without these and other steps, the misfit will continue to grow between the law and the society it serves.

References

Andrews, L. B., Mehlman, M. J., & Rothstein, M. A., Eds. (2015). *Genetics: Ethics, Law and Policy* (4th Edition). West Academic. https://faculty.westacademic.com/Book/Detail?id=31475

Belsky, D. W., Domingue, B. W., Wedow, R., Arseneault, L., Boardman, J. D., Caspi, A., Conley, D., Fletcher, J. M., Freese, J., Herd, P., Moffitt, T. E., Poulton, R., Sicinski, K., Wertz, J., & Harris, K. M. (2018). Genetic analysis of social-class mobility in five longitudinal studies. *Proceedings of the National Academy of Sciences*, 201801238. https://doi.org/10.1073/pnas.1801238115

Chapman, R., Likhanov, M., Selita, F., Zakharov, I., Smith-Woolley, E., & Kovas, Y. (2018). New literacy challenge for the twenty-first century: Genetic knowledge is poor even among well educated. *Journal of Community Genetics*. https://doi.org/10.1007/s12687-018-0363-7

County Health Rankings and Roadmaps. (2015). *2015 Key Findings Report*. rwjf.org/content/dam/farm/reports/reports/2015/rwjf418649

Cyentia Institute. (2016). *Mining for Database Gold: Findings from 2016 Breach Level Index*. https://cyentia.com/library-item/2016-mining-for-database-gold-findings-from-2016-breach-level-index/

Dante Labs. (n.d.). *Whole Genome Sequencing (WGS)—Full DNA analysis for Rare Diseases*. Dante Labs. Retrieved 25 September 2018, from https://www.dantelabs.com/products/whole-genome-sequencing

de Kogel, C. H., & Westgeest, E. J. M. C. (2015). Neuroscientific and behavioral genetic information in criminal cases in the Netherlands. *Journal of Law and the Biosciences*, lsv024. https://doi.org/10.1093/jlb/lsv024

EC Data Policy and Innovation. (2018). *Elements of the European data economy strategy* [Text]. https://ec.europa.eu/digital-single-market/en/towards-thriving-data-driven-economy

Executive Office of the President. (2014). *Big Data: Seizing Opportunities, Preserving Values*. https://obamawhitehouse-

.archives.gov/sites/default/files/docs/big_data_privacy_report_may_1_2014.pdf

Farahany, N. A. (2015). Neuroscience and behavioral genetics in US criminal law: An empirical analysis. *Journal of Law and the Biosciences, 2*(3), 485–509. https://doi.org/10.1093/jlb/lsv059

Federal Register. (2018, October 10). *Inadmissibility on Public Charge Grounds*. Federal Register. https://www.federalregister.gov/documents/2018/10/10/2018-21106/inadmissibility-on-public-charge-grounds

Furrow, B., Greaney, T., Johnson, S., Stoltzfus, T. J., & Schwartz, R. L. (2013). *Health Law, Cases, Materials and Problems* (7th Edition). West Academic Publishing. https://faculty.westacademic.com/Book/Detail?id=2028

Goyal, A., Kwon, H. J., Lee, K., Garg, R., Yun, S. Y., Kim, Y. H., Lee, S., & Lee, M. S. (2017). Ultra-Fast Next Generation Human Genome Sequencing Data Processing Using DRAGENTM Bio-IT Processor for Precision Medicine. *Open Journal of Genetics, 07*, 9. https://doi.org/10.4236/ojgen.2017.71002

Hao, K. (2019, January 21). AI is sending people to jail—And getting it wrong. *MIT Technology Review*. https://www.technologyreview.com/s/612775/algorithms-criminal-justice-ai/

Cook Cnty. V. McAleenan, (US District Court for the Northern District of Illinois). Retrieved 31 December 2019, from https://casetext.com/case/cook-cnty-v-mcaleenan?resultsNav=false

Karelin, D. V., Matsepuro, D., & Selita, F. (2018). Criminal Legal Protection of Genetic Data of The Person: To Statement of a Problem. *Vestnik Tomskogo Gosudarstvennogo Universiteta. Pravo, 29*, 79–90. https://doi.org/10.17223/22253513/29/7

Law Commission. (2018). *The Sentencing Code.*

Lynch, B. (2018). *Dirty Genes: A Breakthrough Program to Treat the Root Cause of Illness and Optimize Your Health* (1 edition). HarperOne.

Malanchini, M., Wang, Z., Voronin, I., Schenker, V. J., Plomin, R., Petrill, S. A., & Kovas, Y. (2017). Reading self-perceived ability, enjoyment and achievement: A genetically informative study of their reciprocal links over time. *Developmental Psychology, 53*(4), 698–712. https://doi.org/10.1037/dev0000209

Moorhead, R., Sefton, M., Great Britain, & Department for Constitutional Affairs. (2005). *Litigants in person: Unrepresented litigants in first instance proceedings*. DCA Research Unit.

Nanau, V., Chapman, R., Metzer, A., Toivainen, T., Kovas, Y., & Selita, F. (In review). *Computer says 'what?!' Mitigating and aggravating factors in sentencing*.

OECD. (2012). *Key findings—PISA*. http://www.oecd.org/pisa/keyfindings/pisa-2012-results.htm

Parliament.uk. (n.d.). *Science and Technology Committee (Lords)*. UK Parliament. Retrieved 31 December 2019, from https://www.parliament.uk/business/committees/committees-a-z/lords-select/science-and-technology-committee/

Plomin, R., DeFries, J. C., Knopik, V. S., & Neiderhiser, J. M. (2016). Top 10 Replicated Findings From Behavioral Genetics. *Perspectives on Psychological Science: A Journal of the Association for Psychological Science, 11*(1), 3–23. https://doi.org/10.1177/1745691615617439

Polderman, T. J. C., Benyamin, B., Leeuw, C. A. de, Sullivan, P. F., Bochoven, A. van, Visscher, P. M., & Posthuma, D. (2015). Meta-analysis of the heritability of human traits based on fifty years of twin studies. *Nature Genetics, 47*(7), 702–709. https://doi.org/10.1038/ng.3285

Ponemon Institute. (2019). *Cost of a Data Breach Report*. https://www.all-about-security.de/fileadmin/micropages/Fachartikel_28/2019_Cost_of_a_Data_Breach_Report_final.pdf

Selita, F. (2018). Unrepresented Litigants in Modern Courts – Ordeal by Combat. *Legal Issues Journal, 6*(1), 35.

Selita, F. (2019a). Improving Access to Justice: Community-based Solutions. *Asian Journal of Legal Education, 6*(1–2), 83–90. https://doi.org/10.1177/2322005819855863

Selita, F. (2019b). Genetic Data Misuse: Risk to Fundamental Human Rights in Developed Economies. *Legal Issues Journal, 7*(1), 53–95. https://doi.org/doi.org/10.6084/m9.figshare.11423724

Selita, F., Chapman, R., & Kovas, Y. (2019). To Use or Not to Use: No Consensus on Whether and How to Apply Genetic Information in the Justice System. *Behavioral Sciences, 9*(12), 149. https://doi.org/10.3390/bs9120149

Selita, F., & Kovas, Y. (2018). Genes and Gini: What Inequality Means for Heritability. *Journal of Biosocial Science*, *51*(1), 18–47. https://doi.org/10.1017/S0021932017000645

Selita, F., Smereczynska, V., Chapman, R., Toivainen, T., & Kovas, Y. (In review). *Judges on genetics and justice: Knowledge, attitudes and opinions*.

Selita, F., Willers, M., & Kovas, Y. (2020). 'Race' and other group discrimination in the genomic era. *Legal Issues Journal*, 8(1) 16-55.

Sentencing Council. (n.d.). *Theft from a shop or stall*. Retrieved 28 December 2019, from https://www.sentencingcouncil.org.uk/offences/magistrates-court/item/theft-from-a-shop-or-stall/

Telenti, A., Pierce, L. C. T., Biggs, W. H., di Iulio, J., Wong, E. H. M., Fabani, M. M., Kirkness, E. F., Moustafa, A., Shah, N., Xie, C., Brewerton, S. C., Bulsara, N., Garner, C., Metzker, G., Sandoval, E., Perkins, B. A., Och, F. J., Turpaz, Y., & Venter, J. C. (2016). Deep sequencing of 10,000 human genomes. *Proceedings of the National Academy of Sciences of the United States of America*, *113*(42), 11901–11906. https://doi.org/10.1073/pnas.1613365113

The Jakarta Post. (n.d.). *Ultimate Duo shields genes, helps anti-aging*. The Jakarta Post. Retrieved 31 December 2019, from https://www.thejakartapost.com/news/2019/03/27/ultimate-duo-shields-genes-helps-anti-aging.html

The Law Society. (2019). *Algorithms in the criminal justice system*. file:///Users/air/Downloads/algorithms-in-criminal-justice-system-report-2019.pdf

The Lord Chief Justice. (2015). *The Lord Chief Justice's Report 2015* (p. 33). Judiciary of England and Wales. https://www.judiciary.uk/wp-content/uploads/2016/01/lcj_report_2015-final.pdf

The White House. (1997, May 16). *Tuskegee Study—Presidential Apology*. https://www.cdc.gov/tuskegee/clintonp.htm

Turnwald, B. P., Goyer, J. P., Boles, D. Z., Silder, A., Delp, S. L., & Crum, A. J. (2019). Learning one's genetic risk changes physiology independent of actual genetic risk. *Nature Human Behaviour*, *3*(1), 48–56. https://doi.org/10.1038/s41562-018-0483-4

United States v. GlaxoSmithKline, C.A. No. 11-10398-RWZ (United States District Court 28 June 2012). https://www.justice.gov/usao-ma/file/872506/download

[USC02] 8 USC 1182: Inadmissible aliens, (2019). https://uscode.house.gov/view.xhtml?req=granuleid%3AUSC-prelim-title8-section1182&num=0&edition=prelim

US Sentencing Commission. (2019). *Intra-City Differences In Federal Sentencing Practices: Federal District Judges in 30 Cities, 2005—2017*. https://www.ussc.gov/sites/default/files/pdf/research-and-publications/research-publications/2019/20190108_Intra-City-Report.pdf

Legal regulation of compulsory genomic registration in Russia and the UK

Nikolay Olkhovik[1]

Law Institute, Tomsk State University

Summary. This article analyzes the legal foundations of compulsory genomic registration in Russia and the UK. The paper assesses the prospects for the development of Russian legislation and law enforcement practice on ethical issues related to the right of access to genomic data, its confidentiality during storage, transmission and destruction.

Keywords: genome, genomic registration, convicts, punishment, criminal record.

Mandatory genomic registration in the Russian Federation and the UK is subject to legal regulation. In the Russian Federation, compulsory genomic registration was first provided for in 2008 by Federal Law No. 242-FZ "On State Genomic Registration in the

[1] Corresponding author. Email: lawtsu@rambler.ru

Russian Federation". In 2011, the Government of the Russian Federation approved the "Regulation on the procedure for compulsory state genomic registration of persons convicted and serving sentences of imprisonment". Under these provisions, the legal reasoning for compulsory state genomic registration is a court sentence that has entered into legal force, on the basis of which an individual has been found guilty of a serious or particularly serious offence against sexual inviolability and sexual freedom of the person and sent to serve the sentence in an institution performing criminal sentences. At the same time, genomic profiles obtained in accordance with the law are entered into the DNA database, and can be processed in order to prevent, disclose, investigate and prosecute crimes that the convicted person has previously committed or may commit in the future. In the UK, legal regulation of compulsory genomic registration has appeared since the creation of the world's first national DNA base in 1995 and has changed more than once. The main acts in this sphere are the Data Protection Act 1998, the Crime and Security Act 2010, and The Data Protection Act of 2018 (which is the UK implementation of the General Data Protection Regulation (GDPR)).

There are differences in the group of persons subject to mandatory genomic registration in Russia and the UK. The Russian Federation provides for compulsory genomic registration of persons convicted and serving a sentence of imprisonment for serious or particularly serious offences, as well as all categories of crimes against sexual inviolability and sexual freedom of an individual; unidentified persons whose biological material was seized during the course of investigative actions. In addition, unidentified corpses are subject to mandatory state genomic registration. In the UK, initially compulsory genomic registration applied only to convicted criminals and defendants. Over the past 20 years, regulations regarding the collection, use and storage of genetic data in the UK have changed. Until 2008, even persons arrested for any crime were subject to compulsory genomic registration in England,

Wales and Northern Ireland. The exception was Scotland, where samples were taken only from persons who committed serious crimes, and samples of persons found not guilty were destroyed. As a result, the national DNA database expanded rapidly and now contains information of convicted individuals and those arrested by found *not* guilty of a crime by the court. This practice applies to children too. After the judgment of the European Court of Human Rights in 2008 that the DNA of innocent people cannot be stored in a database, the Crime and Security Act was adopted in the UK in 2010, which in particular aimed at resolving some ethical issues related to a DNA database.

As the National DNA Database in the UK grows, public concerns about privacy and human rights are increasing[2]. To solve this problem, the UK government publishes National DNA Database Statistics on a quarterly basis; in 2007, the UK National DNA Database Ethics Group was established; government reports of the Commission on Human Genetics (HGC) on the use of biometric data were published; quite a lot of events were held with the public, human rights groups and civil liberties.

The UK Data Protection Act 2018 and the General Data Protection Regulation (GDPR) provide mechanisms for the protection of genetic data, as well as specific protection for the personal data of perpetrators and convicts, including their right to delete information from existing databases if they are not found guilty of a crime; right to correct incorrect information, etc[3]. In the Russian Federation the Federal Service for Supervision of Consumer Rights Protection and Human Well-Being in January 2019 uploaded on a

---

2 Liz Heffernan. The Law Reform Commission's proposed DNA database: issues of scope. // Medico-Legal Journal of Ireland. M.L.J.I. 2006, 12(2), 56-64.

3 Leslie E. Wolf, Erin Fuse Brown, Ryan Kerr, Genevieve Razick, Gregory Tanner, Brett Duvall, Sakinah Jones, Jack Brackney & Tatiana Posada. The Web of Legal Protections for Participants in Genomic Research. Health Matrix 29.Issue 1. 2019.

webpage for a public debate the draft amendment to federal law dated July 27, 2006 No. 152-ФЗ "On personal data" and Article 39.1 of the Law of the Russian Federation of February 7, 1992 No. 2300-I "On the Protection of Consumer Rights ". The bill provides for the processing of personal data obtained from biological and genetic material of a person and services associated with the use and handling of biological and genetic material of the individual.

Overall, the current legal acts in both Russia and the UK do not solve a number of ethical issues related to the right of access to genomic data, its confidentiality during storage, transmission and destruction. It seems that despite the mandatory genomic registration, the solution of these issues should be based on the principles of processing genetic data. First, the convicted must have the right to familiarize themselves with their genetic data. Secondly, convicts, like other persons during voluntary genomic registration, must maintain freedom of choice to use their genetic data, if it is not related to the prevention, disclosure and investigation of crimes, as well as the identification of the persons who committed them. Thirdly, convicts should not be deprived of the right to privacy of their genetic data for purposes not related to the prevention, investigation of crimes and identification of the persons who committed them.

Genetic information under the civil law of the Russian Federation

Elena Boltanova
Law Institute, Tomsk State University

Maria Imekova[1]
Law Institute, Tomsk State University

This article assesses genetic information in the system of civil rights under civil law of the Russian Federation.

In the past few decades, both at international and domestic level, issues related to the legal regulation of genetic research and the legal regime of genetic information have become particularly relevant. In Russia, the emphasis has been on public law aspects, and not civil law. A legitimate question arises as to whether genetic information is an object of civil law relations. The answer to this question is of fundamental importance, since it will allow, inter alia, to solve the problem of the turnover of genetic information (the possibility of its alienation in civil transactions or transfer in another way). In order to answer this, it is necessary to decide

[1] Corresponding author. Email: bes2@inbox.ru

whether, in principle, information is the object of civil legal relations.

Based on an analysis of the norms of civil law and scientific literature, we can conclude that information can be an independent object of civil rights, including, in relation to trade secrets and production secrets (know-how)[2]. Therefore, such information issues would fall under civil law relations named in article 128 of the Civil Code of the Russian Federation[3].

It follows that the same would apply to genetic information as well. However, with the exception of the possibility of recognizing it as an independent object of civil rights for the following reasons.

In legal science, some scholars propose that only information with commercial value should be considered as an object of civil rights [4]. Notwithstanding, these researchers seem to lose sight of information that is an element of other objects of civil rights, such as, for instance, privacy. It is unlikely that the actual or potential commercial value of the information contained in it should be considered as a defining feature of this secret because such information is not known to third parties. It would be more correct in this case to speak not about the commercial value of information, but about its social and (or) individual value[5].

---

2 See details: Prospects for the development of civil law in Russia: plans and modern realities: Interview with EA Sukhanov // ATP "Consultant Plus"; Bogdanov E.V. Information as an object of civil legal relations // Civil Law. 2018.No. 5. P. 29-33.

3 See, for example: O. Kirichenko. Information as an Object of Civil Relations // Modern Law. 2014. No. 9. P. 77 - 81; Inyushkin A. A. Information in the system of civil rights and its relationship with intellectual property as an example of databases // Information Law. 2016. No. 4. P. 4 - 7.

4 See, for example: Rozhkova M.A. Information as an object of civil rights, or What needs to be changed in civil law [Electronic resource] // Zakon.ru. 2018 November 6th. (0.4 pp) URL: https: //zakon.ru/blog/2018/11/06/informaciya_kak_obekt_grazhdanskih_prav_ili_chto_nado_menyat_v_grazhdanskom_prave (accessed 30.12.2019).

5 See more details: Maleina M.N. Concept and types of intangible goods as objects of personal non-property rights // State and Law. 2014. No. 7. P. 41.

Genetic information has both social and individual value, and commercial value (e.g., for third parties such as employers, insurance organizations, sports clubs, coaches, managers and doctors of sports teams, etc.). Despite this, the commercial value of genetic information in no case can prevail over its social and individual value. In this regard, it seems appropriate to establish a legislative ban on the recognition of genetic information as an independent object of civil rights.

Genetic information should be included in such intangible benefits as personal and family secrets. The need to assign genetic information to this particular kind of intangible good is due to the specifics of the information itself: firstly, it can accurately predict the future state of health of a person who was healthy at the time of the examination; secondly, for several generations it can have a significant impact on the family, including the descendants of the individual, and in some cases on the whole group to which the person belongs; thirdly, it may contain information about the value which may not be known during the collection of biological samples[6].

Genetic information may be an object of civil rights in the form of a database. Specifically, a federal database of genomic information is currently operating, the creation of which was envisaged by the Federal Law "On State Genomic Registration in the Russian Federation". By law, all genetic information in this database comes from compulsory genomic registration. The basis of its conduct is a court verdict that has entered into legal force, based on when individual has been found guilty of a grave or especially grave crime, or a crime against sexual inviolability and sexual freedom of the person ,and has been sentenced to serve in an institution executing criminal sentences. The main purpose of such registration is to

---

6 International Declaration on Human Genetic Data (adopted by the 32nd session of the UNESCO General Conference in Paris on October 17, 2003) [Electronic resource]. URL: http://cbio.ru/page/50/id/1038 (accessed date: 30.12.2019).

identify a person's identity and use this information in order to prevent, disclose and investigate crimes, as well as to identify the persons who committed them. For this reason, the accounting of genetic information is carried out in accordance with the requirements for automated processing of personal data.

The legislation of the Russian Federation does not contain a direct ban on the creation of other databases – for example, the so-called biobanks, which collect and store DNA samples, tissues, tumor cells or blood. Due to the absence of special legal regulation in relation to such biobanks, the following legal and ethical issues need to be resolved: what rights do the creators (manufacturers) of biobanks have in relation to the biomaterials contained in them and the genetic information obtained on their basis; what rights should be granted to persons who have provided their biological material, respectively, genetic information about themselves; whether third parties have the right to access biomaterials and information; prospects for industrial or commercial use of biomaterials and information; the nature of relations with other (national and international) biobanks.

Of all these questions, an unambiguous answer so far can only be given to one of them, namely, about the rights of persons who submitted their biological material, respectively, genetic information about themselves in a biobank, and about the prospects for the commercial use of relevant materials and information. The genetic regime of privacy secrets should be applied to the genetic information contained in biobanks, and therefore, the collection, storage, use and dissemination of such information should not be allowed without the consent of the person, as required by the Constitution of the Russian Federation. Answers to other questions should be reflected in the federal law specially developed for these purposes. Moreover, the regulation of these issues, it seems, will go beyond the limits of civil law.

Genetic information falls under the right to a private life (right to privacy). There are no doctrinal or legislative grounds for recognising genetic information as an independent object of civil rights. Genetic data is collected and stored a database as a result of intellectual activity. Additional legislative regulation is needed in relation to the activity of biobanks carrying out storage of biomaterials and genetic data. The genetic information contained in such biobanks should be subject to the legal regime of privacy secrets.

References

Bogdanov E.V. Information as an object of civil relations // Civil Law. - 2018. - No. 5. - PP. 29-33.

Inyushkin A. A. Information in the system of civil rights and its relationship with intellectual property as an example of databases // Information Law. - 2016. - No. 4. - PP. 4 - 7.

Kirichenko O. V. Information as an object of civil relations // Modern Law. - 2014. - No. 9. - PP. 77 - 81.

Maleina M.N. The concept and types of intangible goods as objects of personal non-property rights // State and Law. - 2014. - No. 7. - PP. 40-47.

Prospects for the development of civil legislation in Russia: plans and modern realities: Interview with EA Sukhanov // ATP “Consultant Plus”.

6. Rozhkova M.A. Information as an object of civil rights, or What needs to be changed in civil law [Electronic resource] // Zakon.ru. 2018 November 6th. (0.4 pp) URL: https: //zakon.ru/blog/2018/11/06/informaciya_kak_obekt_grazhdanskih_prav_ili_chto_nado_menyat_v_grazhdanskom_prave (accessed 30.12.2019).

Genomic era and new challenges for justice & regulation

Tatiana V. Trubnikova[1]
Law Institute, Tomsk State University

Daria M. Matsepuro
International Centre for Research in Human Development, Tomsk State University

Elizaveta M. Bezrukova
International Centre for Research in Human Development, Tomsk State University

---

Summary. We are now faced with unprecedented progress in genomic research. Findings can be used for family planning, prediction, prevention and treatment of diseases, understand disabilities and behaviour disorders and to investigate crimes. DNA can be used to identify victims of disasters, locate missing persons, and even monitor trafficking of goods such as ivory or wood. They can also be used to the harm of individuals and society, including through discrimination (e.g. access to health, education) and unreasonable and unjusti-

[1] Corresponding author. Email: trubn@mail.ru

fied state interference in the private life of individuals (e.g. through surveillance)[2].

Keywords: DNA profile, genome editing, genome register regulation, human rights, private and public balancing of interests.

Genomic data banks are growing rapidly. The first DNA database was created in Great Britain in 1995 and in 2017 there were DNA profiles of 4 million people, which is nearly 6% of the whole UK population[3]. But some countries have genetic data of almost the entire population, for example Iceland. Its database contains genotypes of the entire population (about 300,000 people)[4]. *(*Population for 01.01.2019 consists 357 050).*

Created in 2002, INTERPOL's DNA database currently contains more than 180,000 profiles contributed by 84 member countries. According to Interpol's Global DNA survey results of 2008, 120 countries use DNA profiling to investigate criminal cases, 54 of which currently had national DNA databases and 26 planned to introduce them[5].

This year in Russia, the decree "On RF national policy in chemical and biological security till 2025 and further perspective" was

---

[2] Selita F. Genetic Data Misuse: Risk to Fundamental Human Rights in Developed Economies. // Legal Issues Journal, 7(1), 2019.

[3] About UK Biobank //http://www.ukbiobank.ac.uk/about-biobank-uk/ (Date of access 21.11.2019).

[4] Генетический паспорт: что это такое, и зачем он нужен россиянам // https://med.vesti.ru/articles/polezno-znat/geneticheskij-pasport-chto-eto-takoe-i-zachem-on-nuzhen-rossiyanam/ (Date of access 15.10.2019).

[5] DNA can play a crucial role in convicting – or clearing – suspects of a crime, and can also be used to identify missing persons // https://www.interpol.int/How-we-work/Forensics/DNA (Date of access 13.12.2019).

signed, introducing a system of genetic passports or DNA-profiles. Such passports will consist of two parts. The first part will be presented as a raw data in digital format which can be duly explained only by qualified specialist. And the second one is interpretation of this data. The last part will be updated if and when new genetic markers are discovered.

Genetic implications create new challenges for justice, particularly for criminal justice, demanding serious thought, scientific basis and public discussions. Challenges for criminal justice, related to development of genomic research, include:

1. Using of DNA and biological material for the identification of a criminal—raising issues of getting, storing and transferring biological materials and DNA-profiles and regulation of biobanks activities.

An example illustrating this point is the case of S. and Marper v. United Kingdom 2008[6] decided by the European Court of Human Rights (Strasbourg). The case concerned the retention by the authorities of the applicants' fingerprints, cellular samples and DNA profiles after criminal proceedings against them were terminated by an acquittal in the case of S. and discontinued in the case of Marper[7].

The Court held that indiscriminate "blanket" retention of fingerprints, cellular samples and DNA profiles following acquittal is in violation of article 8 (right to respect for private and family life) of the European Convention on Human Rights[8].

---

[6] Case of S. and Marper v. the United Kingdom (No.30562/04&30566/04) http://hudoc.echr.coe.int/eng?i=001-90051 (Date of access 15.12.2019).

[7] Grand Chamber judgment. S. and Marper v. United Kingdom 04.12.08. Press Release - Grand Chamber Judgments Published on 04/12/2008 http://hudoc.echr.coe.int/eng-press?i=003-2571936-2784147 (Date of access 15.12.2019).

[8] 5 European Convention on Human Rights https://www.echr.coe.int/Documents/Convention_ENG.pdf(Date of access 15.12.2019).

2. Origins of violence have multifactorial structure.
3. The recent international studies identify about 40 genes related to aggressive behavior.[9] This means that violent behavior is determined by complex and variative?? interactions between both environmental (social, cultural and etc.) and biological factors. This fact should be taken into consideration in legal regulation, prevention of crime and punishment/sentencing. Also, it poses the fundamental question of equality before the law.
4. Development of genetics is hastening the emergence of new types of socially dangerous behaviour which partly should be subjected to a criminal law. This is especially related to potential misuses of combined genomic data and other big data.

It is hard to find out exact statistics on misuse and harm in medical genetics. However, there is no universal international mechanism to regulate use of data for all stakeholders and so we faced with numerous issues.

There are international efforts and instruments in place attempting to regulate use of genetic data – the turning point made in 1997 when the Convention for the Protection of Human Rights and Dignity of the Human Being with regard to the Application of Biology and Medicine (ETS No. 164, 1997)[10] was opened for signature in Oviedo (Spain) and also known as 'Oviedo Convention'. This was the first multilateral binding instrument entirely devoted to biolaw and into force on 1 December 1999. It has accumulated the effort on the part of the Council of Europe to keep pace with developments in the field of biomedicine and introduce principles applicable to any medical act and «new» biomedical technologies (trans-

[9] Zhang-James, Y., Fernàndez-Castillo, N., Hess, J.L. et al. An integrated analysis of genes and functional pathways for aggression in human and rodent models. Mol Psychiatry 24, 1655–1667 (2019).

[10] Convention for the Protection of Human Rights and Dignity of the Human Being with regard to the Application of Biology and Medicine: Convention on Human Rights and Biomedicine https://rm.coe.int/168007cf98 (Date of access 15.10.2019).

plantation, biomedical research and genetics)[11]. The international treaty based on the fundamental connection between human rights and biomedicine was signed by 35 countries and ratified by 29 as some nations like UK considered it too strict. Provisions related to human genome were also incorporated to the Convention (see Chapter IV). Finally, Additional Protocol concerning Genetic Testing for Health and Statement on Genome Editing Technologies was implemented by the Council of Europe.

Conclusion. All benefits brought by genetics research to various fields, such as medicine, social life and law, have very complex nature. Implementation of the results of genomic research must be based on adequate balanced model of legal regulation and self-regulation as well as high ethical standards both on national and international levels. It requires efforts of interdisciplinary research teams and wide public discussions in order to protect individual, public and state interests.

Acknowledgement: *This work was supported by the Russian Ministry for Education and Science project No.25.8663.2017/9.10.*

[11] Andorno R., The Oviedo Convention: A European Legal Framework at the Intersection of Human Rights and Health Law, JIBL Vol 02, 2005.

Multi-national and multi-disciplinary student groups discuss cutting edge global issues – genetics, AI, and justice

Stephen Aremu

International Centre for Research in Human Development, Tomsk State University

Anna Kniazeva[1]

International Centre for Research in Human Development, Tomsk State University

---

Summary. Leading academics, who spoke at the Conference "Justice in the genomic and digital era", an International Conference hosted by The Accessible Genetics Consortium (TAGC), have explained that there are gaps in the existing laws that guard the protection of information extracted from sequenced genetic data. These gaps are observed cross-continentally. For example, in the US, specific laws such as GINA 2008 and the Canadian Genetic Non-discrimination Act 2017 provide very little protection to individuals. In the EU, even the most relevant legislation to date, the GDPR,

[1] Corresponding author. Email: annakniazeva74@gmail.com

> provides insufficient protection - for example, one provision provides protection and another, counter-protection.[2] The reasons for this include the high economic value and interests accorded to big data, such as that generated from sequenced genetic data; and the fact that this genetic data are needed for different research purposes in the field of medicine, science and other areas.

As a concluding student session of this intensive conference, students had to tackle a practical task. Students with law, science, psychology and linguistics backgrounds were grouped to work together on diverse topics on genetic issues. Students were to imagine that they were members of the Interdisciplinary Council on the Use of Genetic Information in the Justice System. Their goal was to develop guidelines for policymakers on the use of genetic information in the Justice System, using the information and insights from the earlier conference reports. In developing their proposals, students had to consider a number of issues, including single gene genotyping vs. whole genome sequencing; single gene risks vs. polygenic risk scores; gene-environment interplay; confidentiality and anonymity; use of different factors as aggravating and mitigating in sentencing; genetic literacy / expertise of justice stakeholders; and use of genetic information in justice in the era of AI, e.g. robot judging.

[2] Selita, F. (2019). Genetic Data Misuse: Risk to Fundamental Human Rights in Developed Economies. *Legal Issues Journal*, *7*(1), 53–95. DOI: https://doi.org/10.6084/m9.figshare.11423724

Views of inter-disciplinary student groups on actions needed by policy makers

After one hour of intensive discussions, students submitted orally and on paper their proposals which included:

On the legal and ethical implications of genetics

- To establish a global organisation, that would be operated by the UN or similar organisation, for development of regulations for the use of genetic information. This independent body should be multidisciplinary including geneticists, lawyers, policymakers etc., and should have an overarching role to decide when and how genetic data is used and by whom.
- At country level, states should establish departments that will regulate collection and use of genetic information, controlled by international law (which will need to be created).
- Non-profit organisations should be established to represent minority groups, people who do not have access to their own data - to protect these people's human and civil rights.
- To increase education and awareness for populations as to how their data are being used and so that people can put pressure for appropriate laws and policy.
- Organisations who sequence DNA must have a justifiable reason for it.
- One possibility of prevention unsanctioned use is to limit the use of genomic information to state/non-commercial purposes is to restrict the use of anonymised big data to non-commercial state-run projects.

- Regarding data storage: the risk of de-anonymisation may be sequenced reduced if data from individuals were split into multiple sections and stored separately.
- In the criminal justice, in the future, genetic data e.g. polygenic scores, may be used to help with producing individualised probation and rehabilitation plans - to aim to reduce risk of reoffending.

On the issue of using AI in judging / sentencing

- We need to develop algorithms that would calculate or estimate bias in the existing decisions. For a particular case, if the estimated bias exceeds a given threshold, then the case should be passed on for human judging.
- In light of gene-environment interplay, information on multiple factors (e.g. genes and environment) needs to be considered.

On other societal issues

- In education, genetic information that can be used to predict academic achievement should not be used to influence decisions in admissions into educational organisations.
- Potentially genetic information can be used by companies to select employees that are most useful/have most potential for a particular work.
- Genetic information could be used to help inform personalised learning at a school level (i.e. teachers can identify pupils and their propensities for their learning/achievement level), but this would not be shared beyond the school and parents (i.e. should not be shared in official reporting).

- Parents should have the choice regarding whether their children's genetic data are used to inform their educational direction, but this should be done after parents have received some degree of genetic literacy.

On genetic literacy

- To begin genetic education early on so that people are familiar with principles from an early age. This will help to de-stigmatise the issue. Genetics should be introduced into the school curriculum from age 12, at an age-appropriate level.
- To include genetics in training and education of legal professional so that they are able to understand the relevant issues in order to reform laws and policy.
- To provide training for juries and judges to raise awareness of interactions between genes and environment, so that they understand the incorrectness of genetic determinism.

This session provided a unique opportunity to work with participants from all around the world, as participating students came from the UK, the Russian Federation, India, Iran, Kazakhstan, and Nigeria. Work in such a culturally diverse team is a unique opportunity to approach a problem from different perspectives, to see it through a completely different experience point. Different professional backgrounds have also made an impact on the result. We were able to combine approaches that consider the legal side of the question, aspects of human development, and top it off with cutting-edge information from the speakers.

It provided a truly unique experience, as it is one thing to discuss societal problems being a part of a privileged group, and the other - to work side by side with students from historically oppressed groups, from countries with different political situations, etc. The genomic era raises questions considering each person on the planet, so there is time to change, and such conferences are a step in the right direction.

Overall, it is time to rise and make a call for the establishment of a regulatory body backed up by strong laws both at the global level as well as the local level (Individual Countries) to oversee the use of sequenced genetic information. The importance of the interdisciplinary nature of such group's members cannot be overemphasized; a team comprising of geneticists, lawyers, psychologists, medical practitioners, administrators and other professions. It is time for people to be enlightened on information about genetics and how their data are being used. Genetic literacy must cut across specializations, fields, ethnicity and and other groupings. There is need for more conferences such as this.

Combatting the discriminatory use of genetic data

Marc Willers[1]
Garden Court Chambers

There have been tremendous advances in genetic science that will bring enormous benefit to the human race.

But there are concerns that genetic data could also be misused as a tool to discriminate against groups, such as ethnic minorities or people with genetic dispositions to health problems. Such discrimination could occur in a variety of areas, e.g. employment, healthcare, education, the police and justice system and the provision of goods and services (such as insurance).

The concern that genetic data could be used for discriminatory purposes are borne out of bitter and painful historical experience. Crimes against humanity based upon racism litter our collective history, including: the murder of 1.5 million Armenians in the Genocide in 1915; and the murder of more than 6 million Jews and 500,000 Roma in the Holocaust during World War II (known by Roma as the 'Porajjmos').

[1] Corresponding author. Email: marcw@gclaw.co.uk.

Discrimination against Black people and people from ethnic minority groups has its roots in discredited theories about 'race' such as those advocated by the Eugenics movement in the 19th Century. Nevertheless, discriminatory practices have persisted in many States – including, for instance, the forced sterilisation of Roma women and the ethnic profiling of minority groups by the police.

In 1997, UNESCO issued the Universal Declaration on the Human Genome and Human Rights which stipulates in Article 6 that: *'No one shall be subjected to discrimination based on genetic characteristics that is intended to infringe or has the effect of infringing human rights, fundamental freedoms and human dignity.'*

In my view there is a need to update equality and discrimination legislation in States to include a prohibition on the use of genetic data to discriminate which complies with Article 6 of the UNESCO declaration.

In the meantime, there is an urgent need to educate the judiciary, lawyers and the public on the risks associated with the use of genetic data and the safeguards that must be in place to ensure that its retention and distribution is lawful.[2]

In the absence of up to date legislation, the courts can develop caselaw to protect individuals and groups from discriminatory practices using existing laws – though such developments can take time and lead to inconsistencies and anomalies. That said, decisions of supra-national courts, such as the European Court of Human Rights, could do much to advance the protection afforded to individuals and groups in a coherent and consistent way.

There is likely to be resistance to the introduction of legislative safeguards from scientists, corporations and politicians who are keen to exploit the use of genetic data to its full advantage within a relatively relaxed regulatory regime, even if that does allow for there to be some scope for it to be used to discriminate. Such resis-

[2] See e.g. Article 9 of the General Data Protection Regulations https://gdpr-info.eu/art-9-gdpr/

tance will need to be defeated if we are to ensure that the most vulnerable members of our societies are protected from its misuse.

Legal Issues Journal

editor@uklsa.co.uk

http://www.legalissuesjournal.com

The United Kingdom Law and Society Association

To support the Journal or UKLSA in general,

email president@uklsa.co.uk

www.uklsa.co.uk

www.ingramcontent.com/pod-product-compliance
Lightning Source LLC
LaVergne TN
LVHW020235210926
848481LV00016B/2328